The Authenticity of the Early Buddhist Texts

Bhikkhu Sujato & Bhikkhu Brahmali

Contents

Abbreviations

References to EBTs outside the Pali canon are usually from Anālayo's comparative study [2] or from SuttaCentral, unless otherwise stated.

AN 1:1	Aṅguttara Nikāya, Nipāta 1, Sutta 1 in Bodhi's translation [4].
As 1,1	Aṭṭhasālinī, page 1, line 1 in the Pali PTS edition.
D 1	Derge edition of the Tibetan Canon, text 1.
DĀ 1	Dīrgha Āgama (T 1), Sutta 1.
Dhp 1	Dhammapada, verse 1 in Norman's translation [12].
Dhp-a i 1	Dhammapada commentary, volume 1, page 1 in the Pali PTS edition.
DN 1.1.1	Dīgha Nikāya, Sutta 1, section 1 (only used for some long Suttas), paragraph 1 in Walshe's translation [13].
DN-a i 1	Dīgha Nikāya commentary, volume 1, page 1 in the Pali PTS edition.
EĀ 1.1	Ekottara Āgama (T 125), section 1, Sutta 1.
EĀ² 1.1	Second (partial) Ekottara Āgama (T 126), section 1, Sutta 1.
Jā no. 1	Jātaka, story 1 [5].
Jā i 1	Jātaka, volume 1, page 1 of the PTS Pali edition.
JN 1	Jātaka Nidāna, page 1 in Jayawickrama's translation [9].
Kv 1.1	Kathāvatthu, chapter 1, section 1 in the Pali PTS edition.
MĀ 1	Madhyama Āgama (T no. 26), Sutta 1.

MN 1.1	Majjhima Nikāya, Sutta 1, paragraph 1 in Ñāṇamoli and Bodhi's translation [10].
MN-a i 1	Majjhima Nikāya commentary, volume 1, page 1 in the Pali PTS edition.
Mv 1.1	Mahāvaṁsa, chapter 1, verse 1 in Geiger's translation [7].
P 1	Peking edition of the Tibetan Canon, text 1.
RE 1	Asokan Rock Edict number 1 [6].
SĀ 1	Saṁyukta Āgama (T 99), Sutta 1.
SĀ² 1	Second (partial) Saṁyukta Āgama (T 100), Sutta 1.
SĀ³ 1	Third (partial) Saṁyukta Āgama (T 101), Sutta 1.
SMPS 1.1	Sanskrit Mahāparinirvāṇa Sūtra, section 1, paragraph 1 in Allon's translation [1].
SN 1:1	Saṁyutta Nikāya, Saṁyutta 1, Sutta 1 in Bodhi's translation [3].
Snp 1:1	Sutta Nipāta, chapter 1, Sutta 1 in Norman's translation [11].
T 1	Taisho edition of the Chinese Tripiṭaka, text number 1.
Ud 1:1	Udāna, chapter 1, Sutta 1 in Ireland's translation [8].
Vibh 1,1	Vibhaṅga (the second book of the Abhidhamma), page 1, line 1 in the Pali PTS edition.
Vibh-a 1,1	Vibhaṅga commentary, page 1, line 1 in the Pali PTS edition.
Vin i 1,1	Vinaya Piṭaka, volume 1, page 1, line 1 (only included occasionally) in the Pali PTS edition.
Vin-ṭ 1.1	Vinaya Piṭaka sub-commentary, part 1, section 1 of the digital Pali VRI version at `http://www.tipitaka.org/romn/`.
Vism 1,1	Visuddhimagga, page 1, line 1 in the Pali PTS edition.
/	Separates parallel versions of the same Sutta.

References

[1] ALLON, Mark. "The Mahāparinirvāṇa". Unpublished Honors thesis. Australian National University, 1987.

[2] ANĀLAYO. *A Comparative Study of the Majjhima-nikāya*. Dharma Drum Academic Publisher, 2011.

[3] BODHI, Bhikkhu, trans. *The Connected Discourses of the Buddha: A New Translation of the Saṁyutta Nikāya*. Teachings of the Buddha. Wisdom Publications, 2000.

[4] BODHI, Bhikkhu, trans. *The Numerical Discourses of the Buddha: A Translation of the Aṅguttara Nikāya*. Teachings of the Buddha. Wisdom Publications, 2012.

[5] COWELL, E.B., ed. *The Jātaka or Stories of the Buddha's Former Births*. 3 volumes. The Pali Text Society, 1990.

[6] DHAMMIKA, S., trans. *The Edicts of King Asoka*. 1994–2013. URL: `http://www.accesstoinsight.org/lib/authors/dhammika/wheel386.html`.

[7] GEIGER, W., trans. *Mahāvaṁsa: Great Chronicle of Ceylon*. Asian Educational Services, 1996.

[8] IRELAND, J.D., trans. *The Udāna, Inspired Utterances of the Buddha & the Itivuttaka, the Buddha's Sayings*. Buddhist Publication Society, 1997.

[9] JAYAWICKRAMA, N.A., trans. *The Story of Gotama Buddha (Jātaka-nidāna)*. The Pali Text Society, 1990.

[10] ÑĀṆAMOḶI, Bhikkhu and BODHI, Bhikkhu, trans. *The Middle Length Discourses of the Buddha: A New Translation of the Majjhima Nikāya*. The Teachings of the Buddha. Wisdom, 2005.

[11] NORMAN, K.R., trans. *The Group of Discourses (Sutta-nipāta)*. The Pali Text Society, 1992.

[12] NORMAN, K.R., trans. *The Word of the Doctrine: Dhammapada*. The Pali Text Society, 1997.

[13] WALSHE, M.O.C., trans. *The Long Discourses of the Buddha: A Translation of the Dīgha Nikāya*. The Teachings of the Buddha. Wisdom, 1995.

Abstract

This work articulates and defends a single thesis: that the Early Buddhist Texts originated in the lifetime of the Buddha or a little later, because they were, in the main, spoken by the Buddha and his contemporary disciples. This is the most simple, natural, and reasonable explanation for the evidence.

Our argument covers two main areas:

1. The grounds for distinguishing the Early Buddhist Texts (EBTs) from later Buddhist literature;

2. The evidence that the EBTs stem from close to the Buddha's lifetime, and that they were generally spoken by the historical Buddha.

Most academic scholars of Early Buddhism cautiously affirm that it is possible that the EBTs contain some authentic sayings of the Buddha. We contend that this drastically understates the evidence. A sympathetic assessment of relevant evidence shows that it is *very likely* that the bulk of the sayings in the EBTs that are attributed to the Buddha were actually spoken by him. It is *very unlikely* that most of these sayings are inauthentic.

Acknowledgements

We are grateful to a number of people for providing valuable feedback on a draft version of this work. Professor Richard Gombrich, Ven. Anālayo, Ven. Shravasti Dhammika, Ven. Ñāṇatusita, and Dr. Alexander Wynne all kindly provided detailed feedback. The quality of this paper is much improved as a result. Ven. Bhikkhu Bodhi also gave of his valuable time to provide a few comments.

In addition, the content of this work was presented by the authors as a series of classes at Bodhinyana Monastery in 2013, as well as at a seminar for the Australian Association of Buddhist Studies on March 13, 2013; in both these cases we benefited from many illuminating discussions and suggestions.

We also gratefully acknowledge the support and understanding of Ajahn Brahm and the supporters of the Buddhist Society of Western Australia, which has provided us with the time and resources needed to undertake this project.

Thank you!

Introduction

ARE THERE ANY AUTHENTIC BUDDHIST TEXTS? If so, what are they? These are questions of tremendous spiritual and historical interest, about which there is a range of opinions that often appear to be irreconcilable. Traditionalists insist that the texts were "spoken by the Buddha" in the most literal of senses, while sceptics assert that we cannot know anything about the Buddha for certain, and further, that the notion of authenticity is irrelevant or pernicious. Rarely, however, has the question of authenticity been systematically investigated. Seeing the lack of an easily accessible summary of the evidence, we decided to assemble this survey.

There are two main aspects to our argument: (1) there is a body of Early Buddhist Texts (EBTs), which is clearly distinguishable from all other Buddhist scripture; (2) these texts originated from a single historical personality, the Buddha. These two aspects are closely linked, so we have not tried to separate them or present them in sequence.

We consider the doctrinal and linguistic evolution of the texts, grounded in their social and economic context. No particular methodology is preferred; rather, we aim to be inclusive, as we believe that diverse perspectives are useful, indeed essential. So we take into account the internal development and structure of the texts, as well as the results of comparative studies. Multiple independent lines of evidence from the EBTs converge on a point of origin geographically in Northern India and temporally around the 5th century BCE.

But the literature converges on more than a time and a place. It converges on a man: the historical Buddha. It took an astonishing energy and dedication to create and sustain this literature. It must have been produced by an extraordinary historical event. And what could this event be, if not the appearance of a revolutionary spiritual genius? The Buddha's presence as a living figure in the EBTs is overwhelming and unmistakable. It stands in stark contrast with all other Buddhist literature, where the Buddha has faded to legend. Yet none of the later texts could exist without the EBTs; they are the foundational literature from which everything else derives.

We pay special attention to the historical situation of India in the period after the Buddha as revealed through inscriptions, monuments, and writings by Indians and Greeks. Within a few decades of the Buddha, under the reign of the Nandas, the political situation completely changed, from the diverse patchwork of small states depicted in the EBTs to a mighty, unified empire. And from the Mauryan empire of Asoka, starting around 130 years after the Buddha, the sources speak of the existence and wide dominion of Buddhism. For this to be possible, Buddhism must have undergone an extended period of growth prior to the Mauryan empire. This is in agreement with the EBTs, which vividly and realistically depict social, geographical, linguistic, political, philosophical, religious, and other conditions that obtained in a period substantially prior to the Mauryan.

Our argument may be seen by traditional Buddhists as too obvious to need stating, and by some Buddhist scholars as being hopelessly optimistic and unprovable. We reject both positions. The variations and divergences in the Buddhist traditions, as well as the lack of direct manuscript or archaeological evidence for the life of the Buddha, are real and important considerations, which should raise questions for any serious inquirer as to what the historical foundations for the Buddhist religion really are. However, it is overly sceptical and unscientific to conclude from the lack of such direct evidence that we cannot say anything, and that we cannot reach firm conclusions. Science works from indirect and inferred evidence, and the preponderance of such indirect evidence points to the authenticity of the EBTs.

We are not denying the obvious fact that the texts bear all the marks of redaction and editing, and that they have been optimised for the oral tradition. There are even a few cases where the editorial hand seems to have added interpretations to existing ideas. But to assume from this that the literature as a whole has not conserved the central ideas propounded by its founder, or even that it was invented *ad hoc* by redactors, is to lose sight of the distinction between editing and composing. So when we say that the texts were "spoken by the Buddha", we mean it in this non-literal sense. Clarifying the exact nature and degree of the editorial influences on the EBTS is one of the primary tasks of the student of Early Buddhism.

Anyone wishing to establish the thesis that the EBTS are inauthentic needs to propose an explanation that accounts for the entire range of evidence in a manner that is at least as simple, natural, and reasonable as the thesis of authenticity. To our knowledge, this has never even been attempted. Rather, sceptics content themselves with picking holes in individual pieces of evidence, which merely distracts from the overall picture, and discourages further inquiry. Their methods have much in common with denialist rhetoric (see section 7.4).

The field of study we are covering is vast and cannot be adequately represented in this short survey. Our aim is not to treat all items with the detail they deserve, but to outline the basic areas of interest, present as strong a case as we can for authenticity, and give further references for those who wish to learn more.

We have chosen to construct this work in a "modular" form, rather than as a sequential argument. Each section stands, more or less, on its own, so anyone can quickly check the relevant facts on any particular aspect. For this reason there is a fair amount of repetition, and the bibliographic information is gathered at the end of each section. We have kept the tone as direct as possible, and we apologise if at times we seem blunt. Of course, each statement can be qualified and nuanced, but it becomes tedious to preface every detail with "perhaps" or "evidence indicates that".

We aim to give a fairly comprehensive and historically flat overview, rather than a survey of the contemporary state of the field. We believe that, while in certain respects the field of Buddhist studies has progressed, many of the arguments made by foundational scholars still hold good, and that they have sometimes been unfairly neglected or dismissed. The very longevity of these ideas suggests that they may still be pertinent long after more fashionable contemporary notions have been forgotten.

Inevitably, different people will find different arguments more or less persuasive. However, our thesis does not depend on individual details, but on the persuasiveness of the bulk of the arguments taken as a whole. We are dealing with events over two millennia ago, so it is of course possible, if not trivial, to cast doubt on any individual detail. It is only when the facts are seen together as contributing to a coherent narrative that they become compelling. We outline our theoretical perspective more in the last chapter.

The length of the sections is somewhat arbitrary, and does not necessarily correspond to the importance of the topic. In particular we are conscious of the inadequacy of the section on comparative studies. This field is perhaps the most important, and has on the one hand had a broad-based, lasting scholarly consensus, and yet is one of the fastest growing and most in need of further research. Virtually every study that has been done so far, covering many hundreds of EBTs, could be quoted in support of the authenticity of the texts. A survey of the field would in itself be a major research project. So we will content ourselves with indicating the broad outlines and a few examples.

0.1 Definitions

Authenticity: An authentic text is one whose provenance is what it says it is. In this case this means that texts that purport to be the words of the historical Buddha and his immediate disciples were in fact spoken by them.

Early Buddhist Texts: Texts spoken by the historical Buddha and his contemporary disciples. These are the bulk of the Suttas in the main four Pali Nikāyas and parallel Āgama literature in Chinese, Tibetan, Sanskrit, and other Indian dialects; the *pātimokkhas*[1] and some Vinaya material from the *khandhakas*;[2] a small portion of the Khuddaka

[1] We have normally used Pali spelling of Indic terms, simply because we are more familiar with Pali. In certain contexts, however, convenience or custom dictates the use of Sanskrit. When quoting from inscriptions—which frequently have spelling irregularities and inconsistencies—we use the form given in our sources, occasionally supplying the Pali form for clarity.

[2] In particular some of the monastic procedures, such as the *upasampadā* and *uposatha* ceremonies, that are found across all Vinaya traditions [3, 78–79].

Nikāya, consisting of significant parts of the Sutta Nipāta, Udāna, Itivuttaka, Dhammapada, and Thera- and Therī Gāthā. The "Suttas" in a narrow sense are those passages that are directly attributed to the Buddha himself (and to a lesser extent his direct disciples).

Non-EBTs: Abhidhamma, Mahāyāna Sūtras, Buddha biographies, historical chronicles, as well as the majority of the Khuddaka Nikāya and the Vinaya Piṭaka. The Jātakas are non-EBT, but derive from stories that in some cases may even be earlier than the Buddha. Commentaries and other late texts may contain some genuine historical information alongside much later invention.

0.2 Thesis

1. That most of the EBTs are authentic.
2. That the EBTs were edited and arranged over a few centuries following the Buddha's demise. The texts as we have them now are not a *verbatim* record of the Buddha's utterances, but the changes are in almost all cases details of editing and arrangement, not of doctrine or substance.
3. That the inauthentic portions of these texts are generally identifiable.
4. That the above points are supported by a substantial and varied body of empirical evidence.
5. That the denial of authenticity is a product of excessive and unreasonable scepticism, not evidence.

0.3 Timeline

Our dating is based on the "median chronology" [2] [4, 237–259], which places the birth of the Buddha at around 480 BCE. According to the Theravāda tradition, the birth of the Buddha was in 623 BCE and the Parinibbāna in 543 BCE. According to the "long chronology" the dates are 563 BCE and 483 BCE respectively.[3]

480 BCE	Birth of the Buddha.
400	Parinibbāna.
399	First Council.
397+	Ctesias writes his *Indika* [7].
c. 350	Sutta with King Muṇḍa (AN 5:50/EĀ 32.7); may mark final date acknowledged in EBTs.
?–322	Nanda dynasty. First "historical" dynasty in India. Mentioned in Greek writings [5, 98].
326	Alexander the Great in India.
322–298	Candagutta reigns as first pan-Indian emperor.
305	Seleucus I defeated by Candagutta.
300	Second Council.
c. 300	The Greek ambassador Megasthenes in Candagutta's court.
c. 360–c. 290	Onesicritus makes the first mention of Sri Lanka [6, 6.24] [8, 15.1.15].
269–232	Reign of Asoka [1, 367].

References

[1] ALLEN, C. *Ashoka: The Search for India's Lost Emperor*. Little, Brown Book Group, 2012.

[2] COUSINS, Lance. "The Dating of the Historical Buddha: A Review Article". In: *Journal of the Royal Asiatic Society, Series 3, 6.1* (1996). URL: http://indology.info/papers/cousins/node6/.

[3] FRAUWALLNER, E. *The Earliest Vinaya and the Beginnings of Buddhist Literature*. Serie Orientale Roma. Istituto Italiano per il Medio ed Estremo Oriente, 1956.

[4] GOMBRICH, Richard. "Dating the Buddha: A Red Herring Revealed". In: *Datierung Des Historischen Buddha, part 2*. Abhandlungen der Akademie der Wissenschaften in Göttingen, Philologisch-Historische Klasse. Vandenhoeck & Ruprecht, 1992.

[3] We do not regard the chronological uncertainty as crucial to the question of authenticity.

[5] LAMOTTE, Étienne. *History of Indian Buddhism: From the Origins to the Śaka Era.* Publications de l'Institut orientaliste de Louvain. Université catholique de Louvain, Institut orientaliste, 1988.

[6] PLINY. *The Natural History.* Trans. by BOSTOCK, John and RILEY, H.T. Taylor and Francis, 1855. URL: http://data.perseus.org/citations/urn:cts:latinLit:phi0978.phi001.perseus-eng1:6.24.

[7] SCHMITT, R. "Ctesias". In: vol. VI. Encyclopædia Iranica 4. 1993, revised 2011. URL: http://www.iranicaonline.org/articles/ctesias-.

[8] STRABO. *The Geography of Strabo.* Trans. by HAMILTON, H.C. and FALCONER, W. George Bell & Sons, 1903. URL: http://data.perseus.org/citations/urn:cts:greekLit:tlg0099.tlg001.perseus-eng2:15.1.15.

CHAPTER 1

History & geography

1.1 Political geography

The political situation depicted in the EBTs is completely transformed less than a century later.

The political geography of Northern India changed rapidly after the period described in the EBTs. Within a few decades the diverse kingdoms had been unified under the Nanda dynasty, a process that is seen beginning in the EBTs, and which culminated in the Mauryan empire of Candagutta and Asoka. The EBTs must consequently belong to a period of history at least several decades prior to the reign of the Nandas. This locates them at or very near the historical Buddha. Before discussing some of the major changes that occurred in this interval, we will have a brief look at the main Greek source of knowledge of ancient India: the writings of Megasthenes.

1.1.1 Megasthenes

Writing around 100 years after the Buddha, Megasthenes describes an India that is significantly developed from the depiction in the EBTs.

Megasthenes was the ambassador of the Greek king Seleucus I to Candagutta's court at Pāṭaliputta. His writing on India, and those of other

Greeks, survive in quotations in Greek in works by classical Roman historians such as Arrian, Strabo, and Pliny.[1]

The political and economic scene he depicts is broadly in agreement with the archaeological evidence for the Mauryan period, but post-dates the descriptions in the EBTs. He describes the powerful kingdom of Magadha, with its magnificent capital Pāṭaliputta, which was an obscure village at the time of the EBTs (see section 1.1.5). Candagutta had inherited the vast dominions of the Nandas and his empire was the grandest known in India to that time.

Megasthenes does not refer directly to Buddhism, but does notice the *samaṇas* and brahmans, who are essential figures of religious life in the EBTs [2, 98]. His description of *samaṇas* appears to be of Jains or Ājīvakas, although some of what he says may also apply to Buddhist monastics. Clement of Alexandria, writing around the 2nd century CE, connects Megasthenes' *samaṇas* with Buddhists, saying [3, 680]: "Among the Indians are those philosophers also who follow the precepts of Boutta (i.e., the Buddha), whom they honour as a god on account of his extraordinary sanctity."

References

[1] LAMOTTE, Étienne. *History of Indian Buddhism: From the Origins to the Śaka Era*. Publications de l'Institut orientaliste de Louvain. Université catholique de Louvain, Institut orientaliste, 1988.

[2] MCCRINDLE, J.W. and JAIN, R.C. *McCrindle's Ancient India: as described by Megasthenes and Arrian*. Trübner and Co., 1876. URL: http://www.archive.org/stream/ancientindiaasd01mccrgoog#page/n6/mode/2up.

[3] SCHAFF, P. and SCHAFF, D.S. *History of the Christian Church*. History of the Christian Church. Eerdmans. URL: http://www.ccel.org/ccel/schaff/anf02.pdf.

1 Although Megasthenes has been criticised for poor judgement in evaluating second-hand reports, his first-hand accounts of life in India are generally considered trustworthy [1, 221] [2, 26–29].

1.1.2 The expansion of the known world

The EBTs refer almost exclusively to the "Middle Country" around the Ganges plain, while by the time of Candagutta there was a much wider knowledge of the civilised world.

Most prominently featured in the EBTs are the countries within which the Buddha taught, a list of which is found at DN 18.1 and DN 18.4. The combined area of these countries is roughly equivalent to the central part of the Ganges plain.[2] Occasionally this list is expanded to include other known kingdoms, all of which combined are known as the 16 great countries (*mahājanapada*). These countries stretch as far as the north-west of India, including Gandhāra.

Apart from one EBT reference to Greeks (see next section, 1.1.3) and occasional references to the Kambojans, possibly referring to the Persians [4, 198–199], passages on areas outside of this region are typically mythological.[3] South India and Sri Lanka are not mentioned at all and appear to be unknown. Aparantaka, in the west of India, is regarded as a brutal, uncivilised place.[4] Kaliṅga, in the east, is mentioned as a mythical wilderness at MN 56.14,[5] but as a civilised region in later passages.[6] Andhra (Pali: Andha),[7] in the south-east, is only mentioned in the Pali commentaries.

One passage, the introduction to the Pārāyana Vagga of the Sutta Nipāta, describes a long journey by brahman students seeking the Buddha, which begins somewhat south of the regions otherwise known to the Suttas [1]. But this passage, an unusual narrative section of the Khuddaka Nikāya, is probably somewhat late [8, 199].

By the time of Candagutta, a mere century after the Buddha, and even more so at the time of Asoka, the known world had expanded to include

---

2 The furthest west the Buddha travelled, according to the Pali EBTs, is Mathurā (AN 5:220) and the furthest east Kajaṅgalā (AN 10:28), which has been identified with Kankjol on the Bihari/Bangladeshi border.

3 E.g. Uttarakuru at DN 32.7 and AN 9:21.

4 MN 145.5.

5 "Venerable Sir, I have heard that the Daṇḍakī-forest, the Kaliṅga-forest, the Majjha-forest, and the Mātaṅga-forest became forests through a mental act of hatred by sages." Kaliṅga is roughly equivalent to the modern Indian state of Orissa/Odisha.

6 DN 16.6.28/SMPS 51.24; SN 19:15; DN 19.36.

7 Roughly equivalent to the modern Indian state of Andhra Pradesh.

Sri Lanka and South India, and possibly Burma [6, 62, 135–156, 169–173]. Although Persia, and probably Greece too, were known in India from an early period, even prior to the EBTs (see next section), the knowledge of these distant countries expanded in the Mauryan period [7, 368]. RE 13[8] mentions several Greek kings by name [3] [5, 227], indicating extensive knowledge of the Greek world.[9]

References

[1] ĀNANDAJOTI, Bhikkhu. *Maps of Ancient Buddhist Asia: Bāvarissa Māṇavacārikā Jambudīpe (Bāvarī's Students Walk across Ancient India)*. 2008. URL: http://www.ancient-buddhist-texts.net/Maps/Map-03-Parayana.htm.

[2] ĀNANDAJOTI, Bhikkhu. *Maps of Ancient Buddhist Asia; Jambudīpaṁ: Buddhato Asokassa; India: From the Buddha to Asoka*. 2012. URL: http://www.ancient-buddhist-texts.net/Maps/Map-14-Buddha-to-Asoka.htm.

[3] DHAMMIKA, S., trans. *The Edicts of King Asoka*. 1994–2013. URL: http://www.accesstoinsight.org/lib/authors/dhammika/wheel386.html.

[4] HALBFASS, Wilhelm. "Early Indian References to the Greeks and the First Western References to Buddhism". In: *When Did the Buddha Live?: The Controversy on the Dating of the Historical Buddha*. Bibliotheca Indo-Buddhica. Sri Satguru, 1995.

[5] LAMOTTE, Étienne. *History of Indian Buddhism: From the Origins to the Śaka Era*. Publications de l'Institut orientaliste de Louvain. Université catholique de Louvain, Institut orientaliste, 1988.

[6] MCCRINDLE, J.W. and JAIN, R.C. *McCrindle's Ancient India: as described by Megasthenes and Arrian*. Trübner and Co., 1876. URL: http://www.archive.org/stream/ancientindiaasd01mccrgoog#page/n6/mode/2up.

[7] MCEVILLEY, T. *The Shape of Ancient Thought: Comparative Studies in Greek and Indian Philosophies*. Skyhorse, 2012.

[8] WARDER, A.K. *Pali Metre*. The Pali Text Society, 1967.

---

[8] Asokan Rock Edict number 13.

[9] A map that illustrates the dramatic expansion of geographical knowledge in this period can be found at [2].

1.1.3 Greek connections

The Greeks are largely unknown to the EBTs, while from the time of Candagutta there was extensive and close contact with Greek culture.

There is only one known reference to the Greeks in the EBTs.[10] This comments on the different social structure of the Greeks, saying they did not have the four castes (cf. RE 13 [4]).

The mention of the Greeks has been regarded as a late interpolation into the Suttas at the time of Candagutta [3, 353] [1, 551, note 115]. Certainly, the relationship with the Greek world was a distant one in the time of the EBTs. However, there are several sources that mention or imply contact between Greeks and Indians in the time of the EBTs, or even earlier [5, 199] [9, 9–13]. Ctesias' *Indika* was written only a few years after the Buddha passed away [10]. Herodotus, a contemporary of the Buddha, speaks of India many times, and says that Indian troops fought in the Persian army of Xerxes [2, 244–246] [6]. Thus Indian troops fought against continental Greece at the beginning of the 5th century BCE [8, 104]. The Persian emperor Cyrus I had in fact conquered parts of north-western India as early as mid-6th century BCE [8, 102], and the territorial expansion into India along the Indus continued under Darius I in the late 6th century [7, 167] [8, 102–103] [9, 6]. According to McEvilley, the vast Persian Empire, and especially its capital Persepolis, functioned as a cosmopolitan meeting place for people from distant countries, including Greeks and Indians [9, 9–13].

Candagutta's reign, by contrast, marks the period of *close* contact with the Greeks. Candagutta had a Greek ambassador at his court and probably married a Greek princess [8, 117, 220]. At the time of Asoka the geographical knowledge was even greater, with RE 13 referring to the kings of Egypt, Cyrene (in present day Libya), Epirus (north-western Greece and Southern Albania), and Macedonia [4] [8, 227].

References

[1] ANĀLAYO. *A Comparative Study of the Majjhima-nikāya*. Dharma Drum Academic Publisher, 2011.

[10] MN 93.6. For a discussion of this passage see [1, 551, note 113]

[2] ANĀLAYO. "The Historical Value of the Pāli Discourses". In: *Indo-Iranian Journal* 55 (2012), pp. 223–253.

[3] BRONKHORST, Johannes. *Greater Magadha: studies in the culture of early India.* Brill, 2007.

[4] DHAMMIKA, S., trans. *The Edicts of King Asoka.* 1994–2013. URL: http://www.accesstoinsight.org/lib/authors/dhammika/wheel386.html.

[5] HALBFASS, Wilhelm. "Early Indian References to the Greeks and the First Western References to Buddhism". In: *When Did the Buddha Live?: The Controversy on the Dating of the Historical Buddha.* Bibliotheca Indo-Buddhica. Sri Satguru, 1995.

[6] HERODOTUS. *The History of the Persian Wars: A Description of India.* 2005. URL: http://www.thenagain.info/Classes/Sources/Herodotus.India.html.

[7] KULKE, Hermann. "Some considerations on the significance of Buddha's date for the history of North India". In: *When Did the Buddha Live?: The Controversy on the Dating of the Historical Buddha.* Bibliotheca Indo-Buddhica. Sri Satguru, 1995.

[8] LAMOTTE, Étienne. *History of Indian Buddhism: From the Origins to the Śaka Era.* Publications de l'Institut orientaliste de Louvain. Université catholique de Louvain, Institut orientaliste, 1988.

[9] MCEVILLEY, T. *The Shape of Ancient Thought: Comparative Studies in Greek and Indian Philosophies.* Skyhorse, 2012.

[10] SCHMITT, R. "Ctesias". In: vol. VI. Encyclopædia Iranica 4. 1993, revised 2011. URL: http://www.iranicaonline.org/articles/ctesias-.

1.1.4 The 16 nations become part of the Māgadhan empire

The EBTs depict the limited region around the Ganges plain as divided into multiple nations, but within a few decades the region, and far beyond, was united in a single kingdom.

According to the EBTs the north of India at the time of the Buddha, from the Ganges delta to Gandhāra, corresponding roughly to the area covered by the Ganges plain and large parts of the Indus plain, was divided into 16 great countries (*mahājanapada*),[11] one of which was Magadha.[12] This tradi-

[11] Here is a map of the 16 nations: http://www.ancient-buddhist-texts.net/Maps/Map-04-Janapada.htm

[12] See AN 3:70, AN 8:42, AN 8:43, and AN 8:45.

tion is echoed in Jain (Bhagavati Sūtra) and Brahmanical (Mahābhārata) sources, which however give somewhat different lists of countries [4, 7]. Where they differ, the EBT list covers a smaller area and appears to be earlier [5, 42]. While the 16 nations are only mentioned occasionally, the political situation that they represent—of Northern India divided into a patchwork of minor principalities and republics—is inherent to the entire socio-political environment of the EBTs.

Figure 1.1: The 16 nations and the expansion of Magadha under Ajātasattu (c. 400 BCE), Mahāpadma Nanda (c. 350 BCE), and Candagutta Maurya (c. 300 BCE).

Only a few decades after the Buddha these nations had disappeared, as most of north and central India was unified in the kingdom of Magadha by the Nanda dynasty. We have a fairly good idea of the range of this empire. When Alexander invaded India in 326 BCE he turned back at the mere rumour of the Nandas' military might. The domain of the Nandas at this time must therefore have spread as far, or nearly as far, as Alexander reached, which was the Hyphasis River (the modern Beas River), to the north-west of the Kuru region. We also have the Hatthigumpha inscription of king Khāravela at Udayagiri in Kaliṅga, from the 2nd century BCE, where the king speaks of extending the canal built by King Nanda [3]. Thus Nanda had not only conquered Kaliṅga but had accomplished substantial capital works there. The Nanda empire must therefore have encompassed virtually all of the former sixteen nations, with the exception of Kamboja and Gandhāra. This agrees with the accounts given in the Hindu Purāṇas, which consistently say that Mahāpadma Nanda subjugated India under one rule (*ekacchatra*),[13] and occasionally identify the nations which he conquered, including the Kurus, Kāliṅgas, Mithilas, Sūrasenas, etc.[14]

This means that the 16 nations had disappeared a few decades after the Buddha's death, which means the process must have started much earlier. This fits with the picture given in the EBTs. In the Buddha's lifetime, King Bimbisāra of Magadha subjugated the kingdom of Aṅga to the east,[15] and the Māgadhan dispute with Kosala over Kāsi was settled in Magadha's favour by Bimbisāra's son Ajātasattu.[16] By the time the Buddha died, the EBTs thus portray Magadha as controlling the south bank of the Ganges from Campā to Benares, and also Ajātasattu as desiring to bring the Vajjian

[13] E.g. Bhagavata 12.1.9, Viṣṇu 4.24.22.

[14] Brahmaṇḍa 2.74.136*ff.*

[15] This is not explicitly stated in the EBTs, but it seems implied by a number of sources. Episodes set before the Buddha's life treat Aṅga simply as a distinct country, sometimes at war with Magadha (e.g. DN 19 Mahāgovinda and various Jātakas such as Jā II 211, Jā IV 454, Jā V 316, and Jā VI 271). In the Buddha's time, DN 4 speaks of a brahmin living in Aṅga on land endowed by King Bimbisāra of Magadha, thus implying that Aṅga was under Māgadhan rule. The Pali commentaries say that Aṅga was conquered by Bimbisāra and ruled by him (see entry in Dictionary of Pali Proper Names), and regularly refer to the two countries together, e.g. *aṅgamagadhānaṁ rājā bimbisāro* ("King Bimbisāro of Aṅga and Magadha") in the commentary to the Ādittapariyāya Sutta (SN 35.28).

[16] SN 3:14.

republic under his control.[17] The EBTs and independent sources thus agree on the gradual expansion of the Māgadhan state in the decades following the Buddha, and that the subjugation of the 16 nations was mostly complete before Alexander arrived.

Many of these events would have been witnessed by the Buddha's direct disciples, and the rest by the first couple of generations of his followers. Yet not a single hint of any of this has made its way into the EBTs. This is not because they are ignorant of or unconcerned with politics; as we have seen, there are plenty of references to political and societal details in the EBTs. The simplest explanation is that the main content of the EBTs derives from the lifetime of the Buddha, during which the 16 nations were the dominant political feature, and this content was left unchanged despite the political upheaval that followed.

Once they had disappeared, the 16 nations never returned. The Nanda dynasty was succeeded by the Mauryan dynasty established by Candagutta [1, 18–24] [6, 10, 140] [7, 260].[18] He further expanded the Nanda realms to the west and south.[19] This is further confirmed for the Asokan period, when the distribution of Asokan pillars and rock edicts shows that all of India, except the extreme south, was part of Magadha [4, 225–226].

In the EBTs, political and military rivalry is confined to the 16 *mahājanapadas*.[20] But this soon changed: Alexander's army mutinied rather than take on the Nandas. By the time of Candagutta, Greek sources show that Māgadhan military might was measured against that of southern and eastern Indian countries, in particular against Kaliṅga and Andhra, as well as other countries lying outside of the Ganges plain [6, 135–156]. Kaliṅga was then conquered by Asoka in about 260 BCE [4, 226]. According to a number

[17] DN 16.1.1–5/DĀ 2/T 5/T 6; MĀ 145/SMPS 1.2–6.

[18] This is also the position of the Pali tradition. See Sāratthadīpanī-ṭīkā, Ganthārambhakathā, Tatiyasaṅgītikathāvaṇṇanā (http://tipitaka.org/romn/cscd/vin01t1.tik0.xml): *Candakena nāma kira brāhmaṇena samussāhito candaguttakumāro tena dinnanaye ṭhatvā sakalajambudīpe ekarajjam akāsi*, "It is said that Prince Candagutta, encouraged by a brahman called Candaka, by keeping to the method he suggested, made all of India into one kingdom."

[19] Although it seems that he or his successor Bindusāra lost control of Kaliṅga, so that it had to be retaken by Asoka.

[20] Magadha vs. Kosala (SN 3:14–15); Magadha vs. Vajji (DN 16.1.1–5/DĀ 2/T 5/T 6; MĀ 145/SMPS 1.2–6); Magadha vs. Avantī (MN 108.2).

of sources, including RE 13 [2], the Mahākarmavibhaṅga [4, 302], and the Mahāvaṁsa,[21] Buddhism became established in Sri Lanka (Tāmraparṇi) in the Asokan period, apparently with the direct involvement of Asoka himself.

References

[1] BHARGAVA, P. *Chandragupta Maurya*. Read Books, 2008.

[2] DHAMMIKA, S., trans. *The Edicts of King Asoka*. 1994–2013. URL: http://www.accesstoinsight.org/lib/authors/dhammika/wheel386.html.

[3] "Hatthigumpha Inscription of Kharavela of Kāliṅga". In: *Epigraphia India* 10 (1929–1930), pp. 86–89. URL: http://www.sdstate.edu/projectsouthasia/upload/HathigumphaInscription.pdf.

[4] LAMOTTE, Étienne. *History of Indian Buddhism: From the Origins to the Śaka Era*. Publications de l'Institut orientaliste de Louvain. Université catholique de Louvain, Institut orientaliste, 1988.

[5] LAW, B.C. *Historical Geography of Ancient India*. Société Asiatique de Paris, 1954. URL: http://203.200.22.249:8080/jspui/handle/123456789/777.

[6] MCCRINDLE, J.W. and JAIN, R.C. *McCrindle's Ancient India: as described by Megasthenes and Arrian*. Trübner and Co., 1876. URL: http://www.archive.org/stream/ancientindiaasd01mccrgoog#page/n6/mode/2up.

[7] RHYS DAVIDS, T.W. *Buddhist India*. Putnam, 1903. URL: http://fsnow.com/text/buddhist-india/.

1.1.5 The transformation of Pāṭaliputta

The capital of Candagutta and Asoka was Pāṭaliputta, a magnificent city on the Ganges, which in the EBTs is mentioned only occasionally as an obscure village.

Pāṭaliputta is unknown to any pre-Buddhist texts, such as the early Upaniṣads, and we have no evidence that it existed in this period. A list in the EBTs of the main cities of Northern India does not include Pāṭaliputta.[22] While the Buddha was alive, Pāṭaliputta was still called Pāṭaligāma ("the

[21] See Mv 12.78, 13.18–13.21 and 14.1–14.23.

[22] See DN 16.5.17/SMPS 33.2.

village of Pāṭali"; DN 16.1.19–28/SMPS 4.1–4.), and it would therefore have been very modest in size [3, 10, 22] [5]. Apart from a few late Suttas,[23] it can only be traced to this one passage. Towards the end of the Buddha's life a city, the future Pāṭaliputta, was being built at or near Pāṭaligāma, and the Buddha predicts its future greatness, using the name Pāṭaliputta for the first time [1, 202–206].[24]

This fits with the archaeological evidence which indicates that large scale urban development in the Ganges plain, characterised by "town planning, fortification, monumental buildings, the use of bricks etc., does not appear much older than the fourth and even the third century BCE" [2, 165].

The picture found in the EBTs contrasts sharply with the situation about a century later. Various sources, including Greek ones, tell us that at the time of Candagutta Pāṭaliputta is the capital of Magadha and the greatest city in India [4, 66–68, 139] [6, 262–263]. According to Jain and Brahmanical sources, Pāṭaliputta probably became the capital of Magadha under Udayabhadda, son of Ajātasattu, and remained as such until after the dissolution of the Asokan empire [3, 93]. Again, archaeological excavations at Patna/Pāṭaliputta indicate that this picture is historically accurate [3, 322].

References

[1] HINÜBER, Oskar VON. "Hoary past and hazy memory. On the history of early Buddhist texts". In: *Journal of the International Association of Buddhist Studies* 29.2 (2006), pp. 193–210.

[2] KULKE, Hermann. "Some considerations on the significance of Buddha's date for the history of North India". In: *When Did the Buddha Live?: The Controversy on the Dating of the Historical Buddha*. Bibliotheca Indo-Buddhica. Sri Satguru, 1995.

[23] MN 52/AN 11:16/MĀ 217/T 92, MN 94, SN 45:18–20, SN 47:21/SĀ 628, SN 47:23/SĀ 629–30/SĀ 632, and AN 5:50/EĀ 32.7.

[24] See DN 16.1.28 and SMPS 5.12. This prediction may well be a late addition, not a historical event, the purpose of which would be to tie the Buddha to the glory of the Mauryan empire and vice versa.

[3] LAMOTTE, Étienne. *History of Indian Buddhism: From the Origins to the Śaka Era.* Publications de l'Institut orientaliste de Louvain. Université catholique de Louvain, Institut orientaliste, 1988.

[4] MCCRINDLE, J.W. and JAIN, R.C. *McCrindle's Ancient India: as described by Megasthenes and Arrian.* Trübner and Co., 1876. URL: `http://www.archive.org/stream/ancientindiaasd01mccrgoog#page/n6/mode/2up`.

[5] MICHELSON, T. *Walleser on the Home of Pāli.* 1928. URL: `http://www.jstor.org/discover/10.2307/408792?uid=3737536&uid=2129&uid=2&uid=70&uid=4&sid=21101817923573`.

[6] RHYS DAVIDS, T.W. *Buddhist India.* Putnam, 1903. URL: `http://fsnow.com/text/buddhist-india/`.

1.1.6 Absence of Candagutta and Asoka

Candagutta and Asoka are two of India's greatest rulers, yet they are not mentioned anywhere in the EBTs, which indicates that they were closed by the time of Candagutta.

Considering how regularly kings, including the kings of Magadha, are mentioned in the EBTs, and considering how celebrated Asoka is in other Buddhist literature, it is particularly noteworthy that neither Candagutta nor Asoka, both ruling an empire previously unparalleled in Indian history, is mentioned in the EBTs.[25] Perhaps the earliest mention of Candagutta in Pali literature is found in the Milindapañha.[26] And Asoka's life, by way of contrast to the EBTs, is described at length in a number of Buddhist sources, such as the Dīpavaṁsa, the Mahāvaṁsa, the Samantapāsādikā, and the Aśokāvadāna [4, 224]. Moreover, the Dīpavaṁsa (1.26–27 of Oldenberg's translation), as well as certain Mahāyāna works such as the quasi-historical Mañjuśrimūlakalpa, portray the Buddha as predicting the advent of Asoka [2, 312–313]. No EBT contains such a prediction.

---

[25] It is sometimes said that the Saṁyukta Āgama, the Chinese parallel to the Pali Saṁyutta Nikāya, contains a lengthy biography of Asoka. But the passage in question is a mere filing error, where, at some point in the text's transmission in China, a chapter from a life of the Asoka became accidentally included in the text [1, 16, 245]. Far from showing how late or degraded the EBTs are, this incident shows how easy it is to detect such later interpolations.

[26] *Tena ca raññā candaguttena saṅgāmo samupabyūḷho ahosi*, "There was a great battle fought by that King Candagutta." [3, 292]

References

[1] CHOONG, Mun-keat. *The Fundamental Teachings of Early Buddhism: A Comparative Study Based on the Sūtrāṅga Portion of the Pali Saṁyutta-Nikāya and the Chinese Saṁyuktāgama*. Harrassowitz, 2000.

[2] GRÖNBOLD, Günter. "The Date of the Buddha according to Tantric Texts". In: *When Did the Buddha Live?: The Controversy on the Dating of the Historical Buddha*. Bibliotheca Indo-Buddhica. Sri Satguru, 1995.

[3] HORNER, I.B., trans. *Milinda's Questions*. Sacred Books of the Buddhists Series v. 1. The Pali Text Society, 1964.

[4] LAMOTTE, Étienne. *History of Indian Buddhism: From the Origins to the Śaka Era*. Publications de l'Institut orientaliste de Louvain. Université catholique de Louvain, Institut orientaliste, 1988.

1.1.7 No contradictory evidence

It is inconceivable that ancient monks could, after the fact, have composed a body of scripture as extensive as the EBTs without introducing mistakes and incongruities, but these are not found.

There is no reliable evidence, either literary or archaeological, that contradicts the picture given in the EBTs. If the texts that are set in the Buddha's time were composed after the time of the Buddha, one would expect errors in the descriptions of the political situation. Such errors are found regularly in other Buddhist literature, for example in the depiction of Sakya as a kingdom, or in the exaggeration of the size of cities.

1.2 Social conditions

The EBTs depict the emergence of several moderate sized urban centres, a state of development which falls between the purely agrarian culture of the earlier Upaniṣads and the massive cities of the Mauryan empire.

In contrast to the Brāhmaṇas and the Upaniṣads, which portray rural socioeconomic conditions, the EBTs depict an urban life with flourishing trade [1, 163]. As to the political situation, although small scale state formation can be traced in the Upaniṣads, it is only in the Buddhist literature that regional development and struggles between kings are depicted [1, 164].

> "Although the Upaniṣads contain only very few references to socio-political and economic conditions, they allow the inference that their actors lived in a predominantly rural society, dominated by a landed aristocracy and strong chieftains. These *rājās* lived with their little patriarchal courts in a permanent residence within a still very rural context. ... The subsequent emergence of these strong *mahājanapada* kingdoms, which is identifiable mainly in the early Buddhist and Jain literature, therefore would have to be dated in the fifth or even early fourth centuries BCE rather than in the sixth century as we have been used to do till now. A. Ghosh's critical evaluation of the archaeological evidence of the early cities of these *mahājanapadas* (e.g. Vaisālī and Srāvastī) makes such an inference quite likely as none of them show genuine traces of urbanisation at about 500 BCE, the only exception perhaps being Kausambi." [1, 166]

Again, the conditions described in the EBTs fit well with the conditions expected at the time of the earliest form of Buddhism, that is, before Candagutta and Asoka, but after the early Upaniṣads.

References

[1] KULKE, Hermann. "Some considerations on the significance of Buddha's date for the history of North India". In: *When Did the Buddha Live?: The Controversy on the Dating of the Historical Buddha.* Bibliotheca Indo-Buddhica. Sri Satguru, 1995.

1.3 Economic conditions and trade

Trade in the EBTs is generally limited to the Ganges plain, while from Mauryan times there was a substantial international trade in luxury goods.

In the EBTs we rarely find mention of trade outside the Ganges plain. Even luxury goods such as fine cloth were produced locally, especially in Kāsi/Vārāṇasī (AN 3:39, MN 123.18), and then traded within North India. There are some exceptions to this. Kāsi sandalwood, which was used by the upper strata of society, including kings, most likely originated in southern India [1, 79], but was processed in Kāsi and thus known as Kāsi sandalwood (MN 87.28, AN 3:39).

This situation is perhaps to be expected given the political divisions in North India at the time, which may have complicated long-distance trade. There is only one mention of the existence of seagoing merchants in the EBTs (DN 11.85), but nothing is said of where they traded.

This picture fits with the scant historical information available for this time. According to McCrindle, Nearchos' coastal voyage from the mouth of the Indus to the Persian Gulf, undertaken at the behest of Alexander the Great, was done with the express purpose of gathering information about this stretch of coast, and it resulted in the opening up of communication between Europe and Asia [2, 153, 201]. This indicates that seafaring in this area, including sea trade, would have been very limited even 100 years after the Buddha.

The picture given by the EBTs and McCrindle contrasts with the situation in India at the time of Asoka, who ruled only a few decades after Alexander. By this time we hear of trade between India and far off regions such as the Mediterranean.[27]

This situation matches quite well with trade as depicted in the Buddhist Jātaka literature [4, 869, 871–873], which is normally assigned to a period in the centuries after the Buddha. The Jātakas mention trade by sea to Suvaṇṇabhūmi (possibly lower Burma), and also over desert to Sovīra (Rajasthan) and Baveru (Babylon) [4].

References

[1] DHAMMIKA, S. *Flora & Fauna in Early Buddhist Literature*. Forthcoming.

[2] MCCRINDLE, J.W. *The Commerce and Navigation of the Erythraean Sea*. Trübner and Co., 1879. URL: http://ia600301.us.archive.org/22/items/commercenavigati00mccrrich/commercenavigati00mccrrich.pdf.

[3] MCEVILLEY, T. *The Shape of Ancient Thought: Comparative Studies in Greek and Indian Philosophies*. Skyhorse, 2012.

[27] According to McEvilley there was trade between India and the Ptolemaic Kingdom (roughly present day Egypt) in the first three centuries BCE [3, 379]. Ports were established on the Red Sea already in the 3rd century BCE for this purpose [3, 379]. "It appears, finally, that there was a vast network of Indo-Greek contacts by way of both land and sea routes ... apparently this network existed in various forms back at least to Alexander." [3, 384]

[4] Rhys Davids, C.A.F. "Notes on Early Economic Conditions in Northern India". In: *The Journal of the Royal Asiatic Society of Great Britain and Ireland* (1901). URL: http://enlight.lib.ntu.edu.tw/FULLTEXT/JR-ENG/car.htm.

1.4 The Universal Monarch

Since there was no India-wide emperor in the time of the Buddha, it is sometimes argued that the "Universal Monarch" depicted in the EBTs is a later insertion; however, it likely derives from the ideal of kingship expressed in the pre-Buddhist Horse Sacrifice.

The EBTs refer occasionally to the notion of the *Cakkavatti*, a universal "wheel-turning" emperor who rules from sea to sea, justly, without violence. Since there is no evidence for a pan-Indian empire before the Buddha, it is sometimes argued that this must date from Asokan times [5, 176].

But this conclusion is unwarranted [2, 82]. The Mauryan empire probably had a different structure from the one connected to the Cakkavatti ideal, according to which vassal kings were ruled by the universal monarch [7, 194]. Indeed, the Cakkavatti is clearly a mythic figure and an imagined ideal that sits ill with the realistic stories of Asoka and his ambiguous relation to violence.[28] Also, Asoka claims many titles for himself and Cakkavatti is not one of them. Moreover, the Cakkavatti is also found in Jain Sūtras and there is no evidence that the Jains had a close relationship with Asoka in the way the Buddhists did.

Rather, the antecedent for the Cakkavatti is the ancient Brahmanical Horse Sacrifice (*aśvamedha*), which establishes sovereignty from ocean to ocean.[29] Such a notion would have arisen through both the magnification of the glories of former Aryan realms and by comparison with the powerful contemporary Persian empire. The Buddha appropriated the Vedic myth, removed the violent and coarse aspects, and retained the ethical ideal of righteous rule [6]. Parallels between the Horse Sacrifice and the Cakkavatti include [8]:

[28] See Mv 5.20–5.21 and RE 13 [1].

[29] The Suttas ascribe the origin of the Horse Sacrifice to the greed of the brahmans who corrupted the legendary King Okkāka (Snp 2:7, verse 303).

1. The "Horse Treasure" of the Cakkavatti is white with a black head (DN 17.1.13; MN 129.37); the sacrificial horse is white with a black head/forequarters [3, 32].
2. The Cakkavatti has 1000 sons (e.g. DN 3.1.5; MN 91.5; SĀ 264); the sacrificial horse is protected by 100 sons [3, 32].
3. The "Wheel Treasure" of the Cakkavatti plunges into the four seas (DN 17.1.10; MN 129.35); the horse is of cosmic stature, born in the western and eastern seas (Bṛhadāraṇyaka Upaniṣad 1.1.1–2 [4]).
4. The Cakkavatti follows the Wheel across the land and all submit (DN 17.1.8–10; MN 129.35; MĀ 67); the horse sacrificer follows the horse across land and all must submit (Bṛhadāraṇyaka Upaniṣad 1.1.1–2 [4]).
5. The horse of the Cakkavatti flies (DN 17.1.13; MN 129.37). The horse in the Vedas is identified with the Sun (wheel in sky), and is united with the chariot, the military vehicle of the Aryans.[30]
6. The duties of a Cakkavatti and the Aśvamedha are periodic astrological rites that renew the royal and solar powers (DN 26.3–9; Ṛg Veda 1.162, Yajurveda Vājasaneyi Saṁhitā 24.24–45, Śatapatha Brāhmaṇa 13.1.6.3).

References

[1] DHAMMIKA, S., trans. *The Edicts of King Asoka*. 1994–2013. URL: http://www.accesstoinsight.org/lib/authors/dhammika/wheel386.html.

[2] GOMBRICH, Richard. *Theravāda Buddhism: A Social History from Ancient Benares to Modern Colombo*. The Library of Religious Beliefs and Practices Series. Routledge & Kegan Paul, 2006.

[3] KAK, Subash. *The rite and its logic*. 2001. URL: http://citeseerx.ist.psu.edu/viewdoc/summary?doi=10.1.1.24.1805.

[30] According to Kak [3, 2]: "The Ṛg Veda (1.163.2) says that the horse is symbolic of the Sun. In VS (Yajurveda Vājasaneyi Saṁhitā) 11.12 it is said of the horse, 'In heaven is your highest birth, in air your navel, on earth your home.' Here the horse is being symbolised by the sacrificial fire. SB (Śatapatha Brāhmaṇa) 13.3.3.3 says that Aśvamedha is the Sun, while ŚB 11.2.5.4 says that it is to be done year after year."

[4] RADHAKRISHNAN, S., trans. *The principal Upaniṣads*. Muirhead library of philosophy. Allen & Unwin, 1953. URL: http://books.google.com.au/books?id=IxEPAQAAIAAJ.

[5] SIMSON, Georg von. "The historical background of the rise of Buddhism and the problem of dating". In: *When Did the Buddha Live?: The Controversy on the Dating of the Historical Buddha*. Bibliotheca Indo-Buddhica. Sri Satguru, 1995.

[6] SWARIS, Nalin. "Religions and Human Rights: The Buddha's Theory of Statecraft". In: *Human Rights Solidarity* 11.2 (2001). URL: http://www.hrsolidarity.net/mainfile.php/2001vol11no2/27/.

[7] THAPAR, R. *Early India: From the Origins to AD 1300*. University of California Press, 2004.

[8] ZAROFF, Roman. "Aśvamedha—A Vedic horse sacrifice". In: *Studia Mythologica Slavica* VIII (2005). URL: http://sms.zrc-sazu.si/pdf/08/SMS_08_Zaroff.pdf.

1.5 Writing

There are no clear references to writing in the EBTs, while writing was an important part of Indian culture from at least the time of Asoka.

Writing is unknown in the Suttas,[31] while a few references to writing appear in the later strata of the Vinaya [2, 27–28]. This situation agrees with the archaeological evidence, which only attests to writing in the period after the Buddha, particularly the Asokan period and possibly a few earlier fragments. According to Megasthenes, writing was not known in India at the time of Candagutta, about 100 years after the Buddha's death [3, 69]. According to Nearchos, the admiral of Alexander the Great, however, writing was in use in India in 325 BCE, slightly before the reign of Candagutta [5, 11]. These accounts may both be true, since Nearchos travelled no further east than the Indus river, whereas Megasthenes was residing in Pāṭaliputta in eastern India, about 2,000 km away.

[31] There is one reference to *lekhasippa*, "the profession of writing," at Ud 3:9. However, since the prose introductions to the discourses of Pali Udāna have been shown by Anālayo to differ significantly from their Chinese parallels [1], we do not consider this as reliable evidence for the contents of the EBTs. Indeed, it appears from Anālayo's study that the prose introduction to Ud 3:9 is missing from its Chinese parallel [1, 42].

Most scholars agree that there is no certain evidence for the use of writing in India before the time of Asoka, but they disagree as to whether it was known at all [4, 146–152] [5, 31]. Despite the lack of consensus [4, 145–151], the majority view is probably represented by Salomon who says [6]: "... there is every reason to think that Brāhmī [script] did not exist before the 3rd century BC, and that it was created then on the basis of a loose adaptation of one or more pre-existent Semitic scripts, with Kharoṣṭhī playing at least a partial role."

The absence of any evidence of writing in the EBTs indicates their pre-Mauryan origin. In comparison, texts such as the Mahāyāna Sūtras frequently mention writing [2, 29], and this is one among many criteria for dating them to several centuries after the EBTs. It has in fact been suggested that the Mahāyāna Sūtras owe their very existence to the use of writing [2].

References

[1] ANĀLAYO. "The Development of the Pāli Udāna Collection". In: *Bukkyō Kenkyū* 37 (2009), pp. 39–72.

[2] GOMBRICH, Richard. "How the Mahayana Began". In: *Buddhist Forum* I (2012), pp. 21–30. URL: http://www.shin-ibs.edu/documents/bForum/v1/01Gombrich.pdf.

[3] MCCRINDLE, J.W. and JAIN, R.C. *McCrindle's Ancient India: as described by Megasthenes and Arrian*. Trübner and Co., 1876. URL: http://www.archive.org/stream/ancientindiaasd01mccrgoog#page/n6/mode/2up.

[4] NORMAN, K.R. *Collected Papers VII*. The Pali Text Society, 2001.

[5] SALOMON, Richard. *Indian Epigraphy: A Guide to the Study of Inscriptions in Sanskrit, Prakrit, and the other Indo-Aryan Languages*. South Asia Research. Oxford University Press, USA, 1998.

[6] SALOMON, Richard. "On The Origin Of The Early Indian Scripts: A Review Article". In: *Journal of the American Oriental Society* 115.2 (1996), pp. 271–279. URL: http://indology.info/papers/salomon/.

CHAPTER 2

Religious context

2.1 Contact with other religions

Apart from the EBTs, no other Buddhist texts depict the Buddha regularly in discussions with non-Buddhists.

The EBTs frequently depict the Buddha and his disciples in dialogue with members of other religions and with sceptics.[1] This is radically different from all other Buddhist literature, which consists almost entirely of Buddhists speaking to other Buddhists. This difference makes sense if we consider that the EBTs largely stem from the life of the founder, one of whose tasks was to persuade others to his path.

2.2 Jainism

There are substantial similarities between Buddhism and Jainism, which locate them in the same historical period.

The Buddhist texts depict the Buddha as contemporary with Mahāvīra, the teacher of the Jains (e.g. MN 56/MĀ 133, MN 104.2/MĀ 196/T 85, DN 2). Jain tradition places Mahāvīra at 599–527 BCE [5, 130], which agrees roughly

[1] See MN 56/MĀ 133, MN 57, MN 71, MN 72/SĀ 962/SĀ² 196/P 5595, MN 73/SĀ 964/SĀ² 198/T 1428, MN 74/SĀ 969/SĀ² 203/T 200/T 1509/T 1545, MN 75/MĀ 153, MN 76, MN 77/MĀ 207, MN 78/MĀ 179, MN 79/MĀ 208, MN 80/MĀ 209/T 90, MN 91/MĀ 161/T 76, MN 92/EĀ 49.6/T 1428, MN 93/MĀ 151/T 71, MN 94, MN 95, MN 96/MĀ 150, MN 97/MĀ 27, MN 98, MN 99/MĀ 152, MN 100.

with the traditional Theravādin dating of the Buddha. While these dates are not historically precise, this does show that both Jain and Buddhist texts indicate that their teachers flourished in the same pre-Mauryan period [2, 179] [5, 130–144].

Moreover, according to Norman [4, 264–270] [6, 1–17], the EBTs and Jain literature show a number of similarities. And, although the language of the extant Jain literature stems from a later date [2, 179], this suggests that the two literary traditions are rooted roughly in the same period.[2] The similarities include the following:

1. Criticism of Brahmanical animal sacrifice [1, 181];
2. Some ideas about karma, opposed to Brahmanical views [1, 34, 44, 45–59];
3. The importance of generosity [6, 2];
4. Social stratification: the *khattiya* caste is regarded as superior to the Brahmanical caste [6, 1–2];
5. *Paccekabuddhas*: including some of the same names [3, 233–248] [6, 12–14];
6. The idea of a sequence of past 'ford-makers' (*titthakara*), that is, founders of their respective religions [1, 45–46];
7. Shared stories: the Pāyāsi Sutta (DN 23/DĀ 7/MĀ 71/T 45) [7, 569];
8. Shared similes [6, 15–16];
9. Vocabulary: they have a large religious vocabulary in common, including epithets for their respective leaders [6, 8–11], and general religious terminology [1, 55–58] [6, 5–8];
10. Common verses and verse lines [2, 179, 183] [6, 15–16];
11. Stylistic parallels: the use of some of the same metres in verse composition [6, 15].

[2] Some of these similarities could be explained by one tradition having borrowed from the other. Gombrich suggests that Buddhism has been influenced by Jainism [1, 45–59].

The earliest Jain texts often use the same name for Mahāvīra as the EBTs do, Nāyaputta/Nāyasuya, equivalent to the Pali Nātaputta [2, 179–180]. The doctrine of the four restraints is mentioned as being a Jain doctrine in both the EBTs and in early Jain Sūtras [2, 181]. The basic moral teachings of the EBTs and the early Jain texts are similar, especially the ideas of not killing, stealing, lying or indulging in sensory pleasures [2, 181–183].

References

[1] GOMBRICH, Richard. *What the Buddha Thought*. Oxford Centre for Buddhist Studies monographs. Equinox, 2009.

[2] METTE, Adelheid. "The synchronism of the Buddha and the Jina Mahavira and the problem of chronology in early Jainism". In: *When Did the Buddha Live? The Controversy on the Dating of the Historical Buddha*. Bibliotheca Indo-Buddhica. Sri Satguru, 1995.

[3] NORMAN, K.R. *Collected Papers II*. The Pali Text Society, 1991.

[4] NORMAN, K.R. *Collected Papers IV*. The Pali Text Society, 1993.

[5] NORMAN, K.R. *Collected Papers VII*. The Pali Text Society, 2001.

[6] NORMAN, K.R. *Collected Papers VIII*. The Pali Text Society, 2007.

[7] PANDE, G.C. *Studies In The Origins Of Buddhism*. Motilal Banarsidass, 1995.

2.3 Brahmanism

The EBTs depict the Brahmanical religion as it was around the 5th century BCE, which is distinctly different from earlier and later forms of Brahmanism.

A number of facts about the EBTs help us locate them in time vis-à-vis the Brahmanical texts. The EBTs (e.g. MN 91.2 and SĀ 255) refer only to three Vedas, not the four that became standard in later years [8, 166, 213],[3] and they are unaware of the Mahābhārata and the Rāmāyana, which are of a later date [1, 95] [8, 183] [5, 1]. The EBTs depict uncertainty and

[3] The fourth Veda, *āthabbaṇa*, is mentioned in the Tuvaṭaka Sutta (Sutta Nipāta 927) as an forbidden branch of knowledge, but it is not linked with the Vedas.

questioning among the brahmans,[4] which is highly characteristic of the early, pre-Buddhist, Upaniṣads. And while the EBTs are aware of Upaniṣadic ideas,[5] they only name the Upaniṣads once, as Brahmanical lineages rather than as texts.[6]

The EBTs are unaware of Pāṇini, who can be dated no later than mid-4th century BCE [2, 268]. This can be seen in the fact that the EBTs frequently refer to grammar, but as an ancient tradition, not as a modern innovation (e.g. MN 91.2).

The EBTs also depict many deities and practices that are found neither in the ancient Vedas, nor in the later Hinduism. In addition, they fail to mention many practices common to the later Brahmanical tradition, such as the worship of the Śiva-liṅgaṁ [8, 166] and deities such as Krishna, Ganesh, Kali and Skanda.

References

[1] BRONKHORST, Johannes. *Greater Magadha: studies in the culture of early India.* Brill, 2007.

[2] CARDONA, G. *Pāṇini: A Survey of Research.* Motilal Banarsidass, 1998.

[3] GOMBRICH, Richard. *What the Buddha Thought.* Oxford Centre for Buddhist Studies monographs. Equinox, 2009.

[4] JAYATILLEKE, K.N. *Early Buddhist Theory of Knowledge.* Buddhist traditions. Motilal Banarsidass, 1998.

---

[4] See e.g. DN 3/DĀ 20/T 20/P 1030/P 1035, DN 4/DĀ 22, DN 5/DĀ 23, DN 6, DN 10, DN 12/DĀ 29, DN 13/DĀ 26, DN 27/DĀ 5/T 10/MĀ 154/EĀ 40.1 and MN 4/EĀ 31.1, MN 7.19–22/MĀ 93/T 51/EĀ 13.5/T 582, MN 27, MN 41/SĀ 1042/SĀ 1043, MN 42/SĀ 1042/SĀ 1043, MN 60, MN 82.2/MĀ 132/T 68/T 69, MN 91/MĀ 161/T 76, MN 92/EĀ 49.6/T 1428, MN 93/MĀ 151/T 71, MN 94, MN 95, MN 96/MĀ 150, MN 98, MN 99/MĀ 152, MN 100, MN 107/MĀ 144/T 70, MN 108/MĀ 145, MN 135/MĀ 170/T 78–81/T 755/P 1005/P 1006, MN 150/SĀ 280, MN 152.2/SĀ 282.

[5] (a) *Eso'ham asmi*, e.g. at SN 22:59 and MN 22.15; cp. Bṛhadāraṇyaka Upaniṣad 1.3.28, 1.4.1, 5.15.1, 6.3.6 [7]; (b) *so attā so loko*, e.g. at SN 22:81 and MN 22.15; cp. Bṛhadāraṇyaka Upaniṣad 1.2.7, 1.4.15, 1.4.16, 1.5.17, 2.5.15, 4.4.13, 4.5.7 [6, 200–204] [7]. See also Gombrich's *What the Buddha Thought* [3] and Wynne [10, 132–138].

[6] DN 13.10: *addhariyā brāhmaṇā tittiriyā brāhmaṇā chandokā brāhmaṇā bavhārijjhā brāhmaṇā.* Identified with the Aitareya, Taittirīya, Chāndogya, and Bṛhadāraṇyaka by Jayatilleke, *Early Buddhist Theory of Knowledge* [4, § 820]. In his book *Greater Magadha*, Bronkhorst argues that even the early Upaniṣads emerged after the time of the Buddha [1]. However, this view has been challenged, and we do not consider it as established [9].

[5] MURTHY, S.S.N. "A note on the Ramayana". In: *Electronic Jonrnal of Vedic Studies* 10 (2003). URL: http://www.ejvs.laurasianacademy.com/ejvs1006/ejvs1006article.pdf.

[6] NORMAN, K.R. *Collected Papers II*. The Pali Text Society, 1991.

[7] RADHAKRISHNAN, S., trans. *The principal Upaniṣads*. Muirhead library of philosophy. Allen & Unwin, 1953. URL: http://books.google.com.au/books?id=IxEPAQAAIAAJ.

[8] RHYS DAVIDS, T.W. *Buddhist India*. Putnam, 1903. URL: http://fsnow.com/text/buddhist-india/.

[9] WYNNE, Alexander. *Review of Bronkhorst, Johannes, "Greater Magadha: Studies in the Culture of Early India"*. July 2011. URL: http://www.h-net.org/reviews/showrev.php?id=31537.

[10] WYNNE, Alexander. "The ātman and its negation: A conceptual and chronological analysis of early Buddhist thought". In: *Journal of the International Association of Buddhist Studies* 33.1–2 (2010), pp. 103–171. URL: http://archiv.ub.uni-heidelberg.de/ojs/index.php/jiabs/article/view/9279/3140.

2.4 The unity of Buddhism

Separate Buddhist sects, which probably started to emerge around the time of Asoka, are not mentioned in the EBTs.

Although the EBTs frequently mention disagreements within the Sangha, there is hardly any indication of Buddhism being split along sectarian lines. The only exceptions to this are the temporary split over the incident at Kosambī (Vin I 337–342 and Vin I 353–354; see also MN 48 and MN 128) and the more serious split in the Sangha caused by Devadatta (Vin II 184–203, AN 5.100). However, there is no connection between this schism and the later emergence of distinct Buddhist schools.

It is in post-Asokan literature, such as the Kathāvatthu, that true sectarianism is first mentioned. This fits with the general consensus among scholars that sect formation in Buddhism, with the possible exception of the Mahāsāṅghika schism, happened in the post-Asokan era [1, 517–520] [2]. This again points to the EBTs largely being finalised before Asoka.[7]

[7] See also section 6.4.1 on the absence of sectarian views in the EBTs.

References

[1] LAMOTTE, Étienne. *History of Indian Buddhism: From the Origins to the Śaka Era*. Publications de l'Institut orientaliste de Louvain. Université catholique de Louvain, Institut orientaliste, 1988.

[2] SUJATO, Bhikkhu. *Sects & Sectarianism*. Santipada, 2007. URL: http://santifm.org/santipada/2010/sects-sectarianism/.

CHAPTER 3

Textual transmission

The EBTs as we have them now are the result of almost 2,500 years of remarkably accurate textual transmission.

3.1 Comparative Studies

3.1.1 Overview

The EBTs are varying recensions of the same body of texts because they stem from a period before Buddhism split into different schools. They have been preserved in essentially the same form since then.

We possess EBTs from a substantial variety of ancient Indian Buddhist schools, including the Mahāvihāra (modern-day Theravāda) of Sri Lanka, the Dharmaguptaka, Mahāsāṅghika, Mahīśāsaka, Mūlasarvāstivāda, Sarvāstivāda, and others of uncertain affiliation.[1] A century of detailed study has consistently shown that they are essentially identical in doctrine irrespective of transmission lineage [19, 98].

The great Belgian scholar Étienne Lamotte says [20, 156]: "However, with the exceptions of the Mahāyānist interpolations in the Ekottara, which

[1] The only complete set of EBTs is the Pali version of the Mahāvihāra. Of the other schools we possess EBTs in a variety of degrees of completion, from a majority of the texts of the Sarvāstivāda, to only a few scattered Suttas and the Vinaya of the Mahāsāṅghika. In the case of the Mahāsāṅghika, this would change significantly if it can be established that the Ekottara-āgama in Chinese translation (T 125) belongs to this school.

are easily discernible, the variations in question [across the lines of transmission] affect hardly anything except the method of expression or the arrangement of the subjects. The doctrinal basis common to the Āgamas and Nikāyas is remarkably uniform." This is in stark contrast to non-EBT texts.

The basic facts were discovered in the 19th century. In 1859 Samuel Beal published side by side translations of the Pali *pātimokkha* and the Dharmaguptaka *prātimokṣa* in Chinese, showing their virtually identical content. He noted that [11, 26] "... the identity of the code in both cases, therefore seems to be established." In 1882 Beal described detailed correspondences between Suttas in Chinese and Pali [10, ch. 2]. He accurately predicted that [10, XIII] "when the Vinaya and Āgama collections are thoroughly examined, I can have little doubt we shall find most if not all the Pali Suttas in Chinese form."

This pioneering work was followed by a series of studies by Anesaki [9, 1–149], Akanuma [1], Yin Shun [33] [34], Thích Minh Châu [14], and many other scholars. Beal's findings regarding the *pātimokkha* were confirmed in 1928 by the Japanese scholar Ryūzan Nishimoto [24] and again, apparently independently, in 1955 by W. Pachow. Both of these studies showed that all existing recensions of the *pātimokkha*, which total around twenty texts from at least 7 different schools,[2] are very similar in content, with the exception of the most minor category of rules, known as the *sekhiyas* [25].

Recently, in his detailed and thorough *Comparative Study of the Majjhima Nikāya*, Anālayo shows that all significant aspects of early Buddhist doctrine are the same across all extant textual transmissions of the Suttas of the Majjhima Nikāya [2, 891]. Among the parallels to the Suttas of the Pali Majjhima Nikāya, the most important textual source, due to its completeness, is the Sarvāstivādin Madhyama Āgama preserved in Chinese. The Sarvāstivāda and Theravāda lineages must have separated approximately

---

[2] It is difficult to be exact, as some of the texts are incomplete. In addition to the texts considered by Nishimoto and Pachow there are several Sanskrit *pātimokkhas*, mainly of the Sarvāstivāda and Mahāsāṅghika groups of schools, as well as some Chinese texts. In addition, there are sometimes differences between the *pātimokkhas* and the *vibhaṅgas* even for the same Vinaya. Counting each textual witness as a separate source, the Vinaya correspondence tables compiled by Sujato for SuttaCentral include 45 texts, with around 14,000 individual rules.

at the time of the Asokan missionary activities.[3] This means that these texts have been transmitted separately for almost 2,300 years, including a period of separate oral transmission that lasted several centuries. And yet the doctrinal content is for all intents and purposes identical.[4] This shows how conservative and careful the individual schools were in preserving the EBTS.

Moreover, this conservatism must have been inherited from the more unified—both geographically and doctrinally—form of Buddhism that existed prior to Asoka. There is no reason to imagine that the separate schools would all be conservative in preserving their canonical texts unless they had been conservative prior to their separation. Since comparative studies show that the core doctrinal material of the EBTS has been reliably transmitted for almost 2,300 years, the reasonable inference is that it was reliably transmitted also in the first 150–200 years of Buddhist history.

In addition to the full scale study of the Majjhima Nikāya, there have been multiple smaller studies of various parts of the EBTS. These have confirmed that all the EBTS share a similar level of agreement to what we find between the Suttas of the Majjhima Nikāya and its parallels. Such studies have been carried out for substantial portions of the Saṁyutta Nikāya/Saṁyukta Āgamas [13] [16], and to a lesser extent for the Dīgha Nikāya.[5]

Caution needs to be exercised, however, regarding the Ekottara Āgama,[6] which is nominally the collection corresponding to the Pali Aṅguttara Nikāya. Although it shares some significant structural features with the Aṅguttara, the content is often very different [26]. The text is highly erratic and internally inconsistent, possibly being an unfinished draft. Scholars agree that it includes proto-Mahāyānist additions [20, 154, 156] [32, 6], thereby establishing its late date of completion compared to the rest of the EBTS.

This high degree of correspondence among the EBTS across different

[3] For details see section 5.7 on Sāñcī.

[4] Thích Minh Châu's earlier comparative study of the Majjhima Nikāya points in the same direction [14]. See also Analāyo's *Madhyama-āgama Studies* [4].

[5] The following comparative studies are available. DN 1 [15, 18–26], DN 2 [21] [22], DN 15 [29], DN 16 [30] [31], DN 27 [23], and DN 33 [28, 213–217].

[6] T 125, preserved in Chinese translation.

lines of transmission does not exist for any other texts of the vast Buddhist corpus.[7] Even in the stylistically oldest part of the Khuddaka Nikāya, such as the Sutta Nipāta [7] [8], the Udāna [3] [6], and the Dhammapada [5] [12] [27, VIII], there is substantial divergence between the schools. This is despite the fact that these texts do have a common core, which is found across the different traditions. With texts such as the Abhidhamma, despite a small common core [18, 37, 39, 45, 124], the divergence is even greater [17, 151] [18, 120] [20, 180]. But the vast majority of Buddhist texts are exclusive to the individual schools and do not have any parallels at all.

References

[1] AKANUMA, C. *The Comparative Catalogue of Chinese Āgamas & Pāli Nikāyas.* Hajinkaku-Shobō, 1958.

[2] ANĀLAYO. *A Comparative Study of the Majjhima-nikāya.* Dharma Drum Academic Publisher, 2011.

[3] ANĀLAYO. "The Development of the Pāli Udāna Collection". In: *Bukkyō Kenkyū* 37 (2009), pp. 39–72.

[4] ANĀLAYO, Bhikkhu. *Madhyama-āgama Studies.* Dharma Drum Academic Publisher, 2012.

[5] ĀNANDAJOTI, Bhikkhu, trans. *A Comparative Edition of the Dhammapada.* 2007. URL: http://www.ancient-buddhist-texts.net/Buddhist-Texts/C3-Comparative-Dhammapada/index.htm.

[6] ĀNANDAJOTI, Bhikkhu, trans. *A Comparison of the Pāḷi Udānas and the Sanskritised Udānavarga.* 2003. URL: http://www.ancient-buddhist-texts.net/Buddhist-Texts/C2-Udana-Parallels/index.htm.

[7] ĀNANDAJOTI, Bhikkhu, trans. *Ratanasutta—A Comparative Edition.* 2005. URL: http://www.ancient-buddhist-texts.net/Buddhist-Texts/C1-Ratanasutta.

[8] ĀNANDAJOTI, Bhikkhu, trans. *The Uraga Verses and their Parallels; Part 2.* 2004. URL: http://www.ancient-buddhist-texts.net/Buddhist-Texts/C4-Uraga-Verses/index.htm.

[9] ANESAKI, Masaharu. *The Four Buddhist Āgamas in Chinese: a concordance of their parts and of the corresponding counterparts in the Pāli Nikāyas.* Kelly and Walsh, 1908.

---

[7] For details of corresponding Suttas within the EBTs, see SuttaCentral: http://suttacentral.net/

[10] BEAL, Samuel. *Abstract of Four Lectures On Buddhist Literature in China*. BiblioLife, 2010. URL: `http://archive.org/details/cu31924023158607`.

[11] BEAL, Samuel. *Buddhism in China*. Society for Promoting Christian Knowledge, 1884. URL: `http://archive.org/details/buddhisminchina00commgoog`.

[12] BEAL, Samuel, trans. *Texts from the Chinese Canon, Commonly Known as Dhammapada, with Accompanying Narratives*. Trubner and Co., 1878. URL: `http://archive.org/details/textsfrombuddhis00beal`.

[13] BINGENHEIMER, Marcus, trans. *A Digital Comparative Edition and Partial Translation of the Shorter Chinese Saṁyukta Āgama (T.100)*. 2011. URL: `http://buddhistinformatics.ddbc.edu.tw/BZA/`.

[14] CHÂU, Thích Minh. *The Chinese Madhyama Āgama and the Pāli Majjhima Nikāya: A Comparative Study*. Saigon Institute of Higher Buddhist Studies, 1964.

[15] CHENG, Jianhua, trans. *A Critical Translation of Fan Dong Jing, the Chinese Version of Brahmajala Sutra*. URL: `http://www.docin.com/p-22757008.html`.

[16] CHOONG, Mun-keat. *The Fundamental Teachings of Early Buddhism: A Comparative Study Based on the Sūtrāṅga Portion of the Pali Saṁyutta-Nikāya and the Chinese Saṁyuktāgama*. Harrassowitz, 2000.

[17] FRAUWALLNER, E. *The Earliest Vinaya and the Beginnings of Buddhist Literature*. Serie Orientale Roma. Istituto Italiano per il Medio ed Estremo Oriente, 1956.

[18] FRAUWALLNER, E., KIDD, S.F., and STEINKELLNER, E. *Studies in Abhidharma Literature and the Origins of Buddhist Philosophical Systems*. SUNY Series in Indian Thought. State University of New York Press, 1995.

[19] GOMBRICH, Richard. *What the Buddha Thought*. Oxford Centre for Buddhist Studies monographs. Equinox, 2009.

[20] LAMOTTE, Étienne. *History of Indian Buddhism: From the Origins to the Śaka Era*. Publications de l'Institut orientaliste de Louvain. Université catholique de Louvain, Institut orientaliste, 1988.

[21] MACQUEEN, G. "A Study of the Śrāmaṇyaphala-Sūtra". In: *Freiburger Beiträge zur Indologie*. Freiburger Beiträge zur Indologie v. 21. Harrassowitz, 1988.

[22] MEISIG, K. *Das Śrāmaṇyaphala-sūtra*. Freiburger Beiträge zur Indologie. Otto Harrassowitz, 1987.

[23] MEISIG, K. *Das Sūtra von den vier Ständen: Das Aggañña-Sutta im Licht seiner chinesischen Parallelen*. Freiburger Beiträge zur Indologie. Otto Harrassowitz, 1988.

[24] NISHIMOTO, Ryūzan. "Rajūyaku Jūju Bikuni Haradaimokusha Kaihon no Shutsugen narabini Shobu Sō-Ni Kaihon no Taishō Kenkyū". In: *Ōtani Gakuhō* 9.2 (May 1928), pp. 27–60.

[25] PACHOW, W. *A Comparative Study of the Pratimoksha: On the Basis of its Chinese, Tibetan, Sanskrit and Pali Versions*. Motilal Banarsidass, 2000.

[26] PĀSĀDIKA, Bhikkhu and HUYÊN-VI, Thich, trans. *Ekottarāgama*. 2013. URL: http://suttacentral.net/ea.

[27] SHUKLA, N.S., ed. *The Buddhist Hybrid Sanskrit Dharmapada*. Kashi Prasad Jayaswal Research institute, Patna, 1979.

[28] STACHE-ROSEN, V. and MITTAL, K. *Dogmatische Begriffsreihen im älteren Buddhismus II: Das Sangitisutra und sein Kommentar Sangitiparyaya. Teil 1*. Sanskrittexte aus den Turfanfunden pt. 1. Akademie-Verlag, 1968.

[29] VETTER, Tilmann. "Zwei schwierige Stellen im Mahanidanasutta, Zur Qualität der Überlieferung im Pali-Kanon". In: *Wiener Zeitschrift für die Kunde Südasiens und Archiv für Indische Philosophie* 38 (1994), pp. 137–160.

[30] WALDSCHMIDT, E. "Das Mahaparinirvanasutra". In: *Abhandlungen der Deutschen Akademie der Wissenschaften zu Berlin*. Akademie Verlag, 1950, pp. 101–303. URL: http://www.jstor.org/discover/10.2307/410739?uid=3737536&uid=2&uid=4&sid=21102106443137.

[31] WALDSCHMIDT, E. "Das Mahaparinirvanasutra". In: *Abhandlungen der Deutschen Akademie der Wissenschaften zu Berlin*. Akademie Verlag, 1951, pp. 304–523. URL: http://www.jstor.org/discover/10.2307/410739?uid=3737536&uid=2&uid=4&sid=21102106443137.

[32] WARDER, A.K. *Indian Buddhism*. Buddhism Series. Motilal Banarsidass, 2000.

[33] YINSHUN. "Za-ahan-jing Bulei zhi Zhengbian [Re-edition of the Grouped Structure of SA]". In: *Za-ahan Jing-Lun Huibian [Combined Edition of Sūtra and Śāstra of Saṁyuktāgama]*. Vol. I. Zhengwen Chubanshe, 1991, pp. 1–74.

[34] YINSHUN. "Za-ahan-jing Han-Ba duizhaobiao [A Comparative Table of SA to the Pali texts]". In: *FSA (Foguang Tripitaka)*. Vol. 4. 1983, pp. 3–72.

3.1.2 Mahāsāṅghika comparisons

The EBTs are shared between the oldest schools of Buddhism and therefore stem from the period of early unified Buddhism.

The first doctrinal split in the Buddhist monastic community was that between the Sthaviras and the Mahāsāṅghikas. Because this was the first split, some scholars, such as Edward Conze and A.K. Warder, have suggested that material that is common to both these groups of schools be regarded as the most authentic.[8]

We do not agree with this criterion, since, as Frauwallner has argued, "the foundation of communities and the rise of dogmatic schools are two quite separate things" [4, 38]. The separation of textual lineages can happen for any number of reasons apart from sectarian identity, prominent among them geographical isolation. The texts of the Pali school were separated from the Kaśmīri Sarvāstivādins and the Gāndhārī Dharmaguptakas at least as long as the separation from the Mahāsāṅghikas [11, 156–157]. Moreover, the physical separation was even greater, at about 3,000 km.

Still, since the split between the Sthaviras and the Mahāsāṅghikas was the first schism motivated by doctrinal differences, it is worthwhile to consider the material in common between them. This research is hampered by the fact that there is little surviving early material from the Mahāsāṅghikas. It is therefore unrealistic to insist that only material common to the two schools be accepted as authentic. Nevertheless, judging from their account of the First Council[9] and other indications, the Mahāsāṅghika did maintain a version of the EBTs, and specific Mahāsāṅghika literature emerged only later. Moreover, the Mahāsāṅghikas are known to have been particularly conservative in at least some respects, for example in rejecting as Canonical texts that were included in the Canon by other schools.[10]

Known similarities between the EBTs of the Mahāsāṅghikas and those of other schools include the following:

1. The Mahāsāṅghika *pātimokkha* is essentially the same as all other extant *pātimokkhas* [6].

---

[8] See Conze's *Thirty Years of Buddhist Studies*, p. 9: "Where we find passages in which these two texts, the one in Pali and other in Sanskrit, agree almost word by word, we can assume that they belong to a time antedating the separation of the two schools, which took place during Asoka's rule. ... This approach cannot, however, get us beyond 340 BCE with the Sūtra texts, because their Mahāsāṅghika version is lost." [3] And Warder says "... the agreement of these two schools [Sthaviravādas and Mahāsāṅghikas] should establish the oldest available textual tradition ..." [13, 196]

[9] See section 6.1.

[10] See section 6.5.

2. The canonical Vinaya material that falls outside of the *pātimokkha* and its explication is on the whole similar in content in all schools [4, 2–4], although the Mahāsāṅghika text is structured very differently [2].

3. The Vinaya of the Lokottaravādins, a branch of the Mahāsāṅghikas, which is partially available in Hybrid Sanskrit, contains significant passages in common with other early collections, notably the first bhikkhunī ordination [10].

4. The Mahāsāṅghika account of the First Council names four Āgama collections, equivalent to the first four Nikāyas of the Pali, as well as indicating some of the content of its Saṁyukta Āgama. It names all the sections of the *pātimokkha*, as well as other Vinaya matters and the class of *thullaccaya* offences [6, 22] [12, 275–277].

5. Fragments of the Mahāsāṅghika Mahāparinirvāṇa and Caṁgi (Pali: Caṅki) Sūtras have been found in manuscripts dating to the 3rd–4th century CE [1].

6. The Mahāvastu is a Mahāsāṅghika text that narrates the life of the Buddha, largely in legendary form. Despite the elaborations not found in the EBTs, there are frequent references to early Buddhist doctrines. It also contains several dozens of Suttas, verses, and passages in a form little different from the EBTs [7, ch. 2].

7. The school of the Ekottara Āgama preserved in Chinese is problematic, although some scholars cautiously ascribe it to the Mahāsāṅghikas. In any case, while the text is erratic, inconsistent—both internally and with the EBTs as a whole—and contains much material that belongs to non-EBT literature, such as proto-Mahāyāna ideas [5, 154, 156], most of the basic doctrine and many of the texts are similar to other EBTs.

8. The Śālistamba Sūtra is an early Mahāyāna Sūtra that is thought by Reat to derive from the Mahāsāṅghika school [9]. This Sutta contains many phrases and ideas on dependent origination that are

found in identical terms in all the EBTs, while at the same time developing these ideas in new ways [8, 27–28]. This too shows that the Mahāsāṅghikas had their own version of the EBTs, which was essentially the same as that of the other schools.

References

[1] BRAARVIG, Jens et al., eds. *Buddhist manuscripts of the Schøyen collection vol. I*. Hermes Academic Publishing, 2000. URL: http://www.hermesac.no/Prospect_Hermes_100806.pdf.

[2] CLARKE, Shayne. "Vinaya Mātṛkā—Mother of the Monastic Codes, or Just Another Set of Lists? A Response to Frauwallner's Handling of the Mahāsaṁghika Vinaya". In: *Indo-Iranian Journal* 47 (2004), pp. 77–120.

[3] CONZE, Edward. *Thirty Years of Buddhist Studies*. 1967. URL: http://lirs.ru/lib/conze/Thirty_Years_of_Buddhist_studies,Conze,1967,incomplete,300dpi.pdf.

[4] FRAUWALLNER, E. *The Earliest Vinaya and the Beginnings of Buddhist Literature*. Serie Orientale Roma. Istituto Italiano per il Medio ed Estremo Oriente, 1956.

[5] LAMOTTE, Étienne. *History of Indian Buddhism: From the Origins to the Śaka Era*. Publications de l'Institut orientaliste de Louvain. Université catholique de Louvain, Institut orientaliste, 1988.

[6] PACHOW, W. *A Comparative Study of the Pratimoksha: On the Basis of its Chinese, Tibetan, Sanskrit and Pali Versions*. Motilal Banarsidass, 2000.

[7] RAHULA, Bhikkhu Telwatte. *A Critical Study of the Mahāvastu*. Motilal Banarsidass, 1978.

[8] REAT, Noble Ross. "The Historical Buddha and his Teachings". In: *Encyclopedia of Indian Philosophy*. Ed. by POTTER, Karl H. Vol. VII: Abhidharma Buddhism to 150 AD. Motilal Banarsidass, 1996, pp. 3–57.

[9] REAT, Noble Ross, trans. *The Śālistamba Sūtra*. Motilal Banarsidass, 1993.

[10] ROTH, Gustav, trans. *Bhikṣuṇī-vinaya: manual of discipline for Buddhist nuns*. Bhoṭadeśīya-Saṁskṛta-granthamālā. K.P. Jayaswal Research Institute, 1970.

[11] SUJATO, Bhikkhu. *Sects & Sectarianism*. Santipada, 2007. URL: http://santifm.org/santipada/2010/sects-sectarianism/.

[12] SUZUKI, Teitaro. "The First Buddhist Council". In: *The Monist* XIV (1904). URL: http://www.sacred-texts.com/journals/mon/1stbudcn.htm.

[13] WARDER, A.K. *Indian Buddhism*. Buddhism Series. Motilal Banarsidass, 2000.

3.1.3 Later borrowing

The similarities between the EBTs cannot be a result of later borrowing, since known cases of later borrowing do not show the pervasive and consistent similarities found between different recensions of the EBTs.

Schopen suggests that the shared content of the EBTs may be due to later borrowing, levelling, and standardisation [9, 80]. However, as recently shown by Anālayo, there is no evidence for this [1, 225–233]. At the same time, there is much evidence to the contrary. Moreover, the thesis of a shared origin is simpler, more natural, and more powerful than that of later borrowing.

Wynne has given some specific examples where later borrowing is very unlikely to have taken place, especially where incidental details are found shared between totally distinct types of texts or where the shared material, although irrelevant to any point of Buddhist doctrine, is counter to the usual Sutta presentation [10, 59–65]. But the argument against later borrowing is not limited to a few specific examples.

Consider the Vinaya. Here we have a clearly demarcated text, where the *pātimokkha* is obviously older than the *vibhaṅga* material that surrounds it [3, 143] [5, 68–69] [7, XVI–XX] [8, 3]. The *pātimokkha* is almost identical across every school [8], while the *vibhaṅga* material is substantially different [5, 66] [6, 165]. If the later borrowing thesis were correct, one would not expect this difference in standardisation between the *pātimokkha* and the *vibhaṅga*. Thus the "shared origin" thesis is confirmed.

This is not just a characteristic of the Vinaya, but applies to every Buddhist text we have available for comparison. The Abhidhammas of various schools, to give another example, diverge far more than the EBTs, but what they have in common is especially those passages that quote the EBTs [4, 19].

Moreover, we have many examples of actual borrowing among non-EBTs and these compare very differently from parallel texts among the EBTs. For instance, the Buddha legend shows many signs of shared borrowings between the schools, but these are borrowings of ideas, episodes, and motifs, not the massive sharing of thousands of nearly identical texts, which would be required to explain the existence of the EBTs by means of borrowing.

Likewise, the Jātakas, and many other Buddhist stories, frequently appear to have been borrowed across the traditions, but the resulting similarities are quite different from those within the EBTs.

In the realm of philosophy, we also find borrowing. For example, key Abhidhammic ideas such as *svabhāva/sabhāva*, *svalakṣaṇa/salakkhaṇa*, and *sāmānyalakṣaṇa/sāmaññalakkhaṇa* are shared between the Pali, Sarvāstivādin, and other Abhidhamma systems, and are defined in similar ways.[11] Yet the texts and philosophies in which the term appears differ widely depending on the school.

There are, therefore, many well-known examples of later borrowing between the schools, and the results of such borrowings are all quite different from the sort of uniformity we see between the EBTs.

References

[1] ANĀLAYO. "The Historical Value of the Pāli Discourses". In: *Indo-Iranian Journal* 55 (2012), pp. 223–253.

[2] DHAMMAJOTI, K.L. *Sarvāstivāda Abhidharma*. Centre for Buddhist Studies, 2002.

[3] FRAUWALLNER, E. *The Earliest Vinaya and the Beginnings of Buddhist Literature*. Serie Orientale Roma. Istituto Italiano per il Medio ed Estremo Oriente, 1956.

[4] FRAUWALLNER, E., KIDD, S.F., and STEINKELLNER, E. *Studies in Abhidharma Literature and the Origins of Buddhist Philosophical Systems*. SUNY Series in Indian Thought. State University of New York Press, 1995.

[5] HINÜBER, Oskar VON. *Selected papers on Pali studies*. The Pali Text Society, 1994.

[11] Compare, for example, the basic Abhidhamma definition of a *dhamma*. Theravāda: "*attano pana sabhāvaṁ dhārentīti dhammā*", "they are dhammas because they carry their own intrinsic essence" (Aṭṭhasālinī, Tikamātikāpadavaṇṇanā (http://www.tipitaka.org/romn/). Sarvāstivāda: "*svalakṣaṇadhāraṇād dharmaḥ*", "a dharma is that which carries its own characteristic" [2, 2.3.1–2].

[6] LAMOTTE, Étienne. *History of Indian Buddhism: From the Origins to the Śaka Era.* Publications de l'Institut orientaliste de Louvain. Université catholique de Louvain, Institut orientaliste, 1988.

[7] OLDENBERG, H., ed. *Vinaya Piṭaka.* Pali Text Society, 1879–1883.

[8] PACHOW, W. *A Comparative Study of the Pratimoksha: On the Basis of its Chinese, Tibetan, Sanskrit and Pali Versions.* Motilal Banarsidass, 2000.

[9] SCHOPEN, Gregory. *Bones, Stones, and Buddhist Monks.* University of Hawai'i Press, 1997.

[10] WYNNE, Alexander. "The Historical Authenticity of Early Buddhist Literature". In: *Vienna Journal of South Asian Studies* XLIX (2005), pp. 35–70. URL: http://www.ocbs.org/images/stories/awynne2005wzks.pdf.

3.2 The reliability of the oral tradition

There is strong evidence that the oral tradition, as developed in Buddhism, was highly reliable.

For several hundred years, from the time that separate transmission lineages emerged in the Asokan period until the texts were written down, the EBTs were passed down orally in separate textual lineages. Comparative studies have shown that this oral transmission was highly reliable and that the core doctrinal material was essentially unchanged. How did this work, given what we know about the unreliability of memory? Indian culture provided the template for highly reliable oral preservation. It is known that the Ṛg Veda and other Vedic texts were transmitted orally—that is, by memory—with extreme accuracy for over two thousand years [5, 102] [8, 240].

In his comprehensive study of the Majjhima Nikāya, Anālayo considers the impact of oral transmission and concludes: "At the same time, rather than giving us a completely new picture of early Buddhism, what my comparative study of the parallels to the Majjhima Nikāya discourses yields is a reconfirmation of the essentials, with occasional divergence in details." [2, 891]

In the field of oral literature, there is a distinction between texts that are to be memorised verbatim, as in the Buddhist and Vedic traditions, and those which serve as springboards for storytelling, as in oral folk traditions.

The latter are subject to natural evolution and variation; they are meant to adapt to the teller and the situation [2, 17]. Such, according to Oldenberg, are also found in Buddhist literature, specifically in the Jātaka collection of the Khuddaka Nikāya [7, 19, 23]. But the former, which are codified and fixed texts, are meant to be preserved in exact form, as in the case of the EBTs [9].[12]

The Indian oral culture developed various methods to ensure that this was achieved. Such methods pervade every aspect of the EBTs, and include [2, 11–17]:

1. Repetitions of words, phrases, passages and whole Suttas;
2. Standardisation of words, phrases and passages;
3. The use of synonyms;
4. The use of the waxing syllable principle [1];
5. Sound similarities;
6. Concatenation of Suttas or other textual units [6, § 21];
7. Formal structures, especially ABA;[13]
8. "Summary" and "exposition", which is a standard feature of Indian oral education;
9. Framing narratives to define the limits and give the context for the spoken material;
10. Verse summaries of prose teachings (especially in the Aṅguttara);

---

[12] Lance Cousins, however, argues that the early Buddhist oral tradition to some extent was characterised by improvisation [4]. This seems unlikely to us given that the EBTs themselves emphasise verbatim recollection (MN 103.5-8) and group recitation (DN 29.17): 'meaning with meaning and phrase with phrase should be recited together', *atthena attham vyanjanena vyanjanam sangayitabbam*. Group recitation is also mentioned at DN 33.7; Vin I 169; Vin II 75; Vin II 185-186; Vin III 159). Improvisation is not possible in these circumstances. For a detailed response to Cousins see [3].

[13] For instance a doctrinal passage followed by a simile followed by a verbatim repetition of the doctrinal passage.

11. Similes (usually in an ABA structure);
12. Numbered lists;
13. Group recitals [1, 366].

References

[1] ALLON, Mark. *Style and Function: A Study of the Dominant Stylistic Features of the Prose Portions of Pāli Canonical Sutta Texts and Their Mnemonic Function.* Studia Philologica Buddhica: Monographs Series. International Institute for Buddhist Studies of the International College for Advanced Buddhist Studies, 1997.

[2] ANĀLAYO. *A Comparative Study of the Majjhima-nikāya.* Dharma Drum Academic Publisher, 2011.

[3] ANĀLAYO. "The Brahmajāla and the Early Buddhist Oral Tradition". In: *Annual Report of the International Research Institute for Advanced Buddhology at Soka University (ARIRIAB).* Vol. XVII. 2014, forthcoming.

[4] COUSINS, Lance. "Pali Oral Literature". In: *Buddhist Studies Ancient and Modern.* Curzon Press, 1983, pp. 1–11.

[5] GOMBRICH, Richard. *What the Buddha Thought.* Oxford Centre for Buddhist Studies monographs. Equinox, 2009.

[6] HINÜBER, Oskar VON. *A Handbook of Pāli Literature.* Indian philology and South Asian studies. Walter de Gruyter, 2000.

[7] OLDENBERG, H. "The Prose-and-Verse Type of Narrative and the Jātakas". In: *Journal of the Pali Text Society* VI (1908–12), pp. 19–50.

[8] SCHARFE, H. *Handbook of Oriental Studies.* V. 16. Brill, 2002.

[9] WYNNE, Alexander. "The Oral Transmission of the Early Buddhist Literature". In: *Journal of the International Association of Buddhist Studies* 27.1 (2004), pp. 97–127. URL: http://archiv.ub.uni-heidelberg.de/ojs/index.php/jiabs/article/view/8945/2838.

3.3 A democracy of conservatism

The structure of the Buddhist Sangha, which was the guardian of the texts, inherently favours conservatism in regard to the preservation of the teachings.

Unlike most religious organisations, the Sangha has traditionally not had a clear and established hierarchy, and after the Buddha there has never been a person of final authority, a sole arbiter of power.[14] Instead, the Sangha has been decentralised and the texts were passed down through group recital (*saṅgīti*). This is the method recommended by the EBTs themselves for preserving the teachings.[15]

This means that no individual, or sub-Sangha group, would have been able to exert much influence on the content of the texts [2, 26–27] [3, 20] [4, 254]. It is thus improbable that the doctrinal core of the EBTs was deliberately changed [1, 888].

The differences between the recensions generally stem from editorial choices in the organisation and structure of the texts, as well as occasional inconsequential errors that arose during oral transmission [1, 890]. Doctrinal development, by contrast, happened by way of new texts and interpretations, and were not due to deliberate alterations of the EBTs.

References

[1] ANĀLAYO. *A Comparative Study of the Majjhima-nikāya*. Dharma Drum Academic Publisher, 2011.

[2] GOMBRICH, Richard. “How the Mahayana Began”. In: *Buddhist Forum* I (2012), pp. 21–30. URL: http://www.shin-ibs.edu/documents/bForum/v1/01Gombrich.pdf.

[3] GOMBRICH, Richard. *Theravāda Buddhism: A Social History from Ancient Benares to Modern Colombo*. The Library of Religious Beliefs and Practices Series. Routledge & Kegan Paul, 2006.

[4] MCMAHAN, David. “Orality, Writing, and Authority in South Asian Buddhism: Visionary Literature and the Struggle for Legitimacy in the Mahāyāna”. In: *History of Religions* 37 (1998), pp. 249–274. URL: http://ccbs.ntu.edu.tw/FULLTEXT/JR-EPT/mc.htm.

[14] See DN 16.2.25–26/SMPS 14.10–11 and MN 108.7–9/MĀ 145.

[15] See DN 29.17, DN 33.1.7 and MN 103.4–8.

3.4 How to make it up

Two passages in the Vinayas that give instructions on how to "make up" texts have been adduced as evidence for the unreliability of the traditions, but these passages refer to the standardising of background details, not to the doctrinal content.

There are a couple of passages in the Vinayas that give instructions on how to add missing material.[16] For example, if the city where a discourse was spoken is unknown, it should be said that it took place in one of the six great cities mentioned in the EBTs.

This merely confirms what was known to Buddhist scholars already: that many of the incidental details in the texts have arisen from an artificial standardisation. This incidental detail, the framing narrative, must in all cases have been added after the Sutta was spoken [2, 22].

This is confirmed by the tradition that at the First Council Mahākassapa asked Ānanda about the location, subject matter, protagonist and background story for each Sutta. These questions would have been superfluous if the Suttas already contained the narrative material. And the new material was not added to the substance of the text.[17]

The purpose of adding this material was to preserve the text by creating a "container" that gave the text a clear and separate identity [4]. Schopen's representation of this process as "If You Can't Remember, How to Make It Up: Some Monastic Rules For Redacting Canonical Texts" is grossly misleading [3, 395–407].

References

[1] ANĀLAYO. *A Comparative Study of the Majjhima-nikāya*. Dharma Drum Academic Publisher, 2011.

[16] The Mahāsāṅghika Vinaya at T1425, 497a6; and the Mūlasarvāstivāda Vinaya at T1451, 328c15 and T1458, 575b29. The corresponding passage in the Tibetan (Mūlasarvāstivāda) Vinaya (Dul'ba, da 39b3) is translated and discussed by Schopen in *Buddhist Monks and Business Matters* [3, 395–407].

[17] That the narrative material stands apart from the rest of the Sutta is also clear from some of the linguistic forms it contains. One obvious example is the narrative form *bhikkhavo* versus the standard Sutta form *bhikkhave*. Another is the use of the vocative form *bhadante* to address the Buddha versus the usual Sutta form *bhante* [1, 21–22].

[2] GOMBRICH, Richard. "How the Mahayana Began". In: *Buddhist Forum* I (2012), pp. 21–30. URL: http://www.shin-ibs.edu/documents/bForum/v1/01Gombrich.pdf.

[3] SCHOPEN, Gregory. *Buddhist Monks and Business Matters: Still More Papers on Monastic Buddhism in India*. Studies in the Buddhist Tradition. University of Hawai'i Press, 2004.

[4] SUJATO, Bhikkhu. *Concerning baskets*. 26 December 2012. URL: http://sujato.wordpress.com/2012/12/26/concerning-baskets/.

3.5 The age of Pali

Pali is closely related to the language spoken by the historical Buddha, and there are hardly any indications of linguistic differences between the two that might affect the meaning of the texts.

Early generations of Indologists accepted the traditional Theravādin claim that Pali was the language of the Buddha. More recent linguistic studies, however, show that Pali is in part an artificial language, created some time after the Buddha [3, 140]. However, the differences in language between Pali and the historically datable language of the Asokan pillars are no more than minor phonetic changes that rarely, if ever, affect the meaning of the content. In all probability a similarly close relationship obtains between Pali and the historical Buddha's own dialect [2, 194] [9, 11].[18]

Moreover, the Buddha himself may have used varying dialects depending on where he travelled [2, 190–191] [5, 99], and certainly his disciples did: they were in fact encouraged to speak in their own dialect.[19] As Buddhism spread throughout Northern India, this diverging use of language must eventually have led to a need for standardisation, and this probably explains the introduction and development of Pali. Alternatively, or perhaps complementarily, Pali is related to a particular dialect in India from

[18] Assuming a span of 150 years between the Buddha and the date of the Asokan inscriptions, one may compare contemporary English with the English of the mid-19th century. Generally speaking, and despite the pressures on English from a progressive globalisation, the English of around 1850 is perfectly comprehensible and unambiguous to a modern reader.

[19] MN 139.12/MĀ 169 and Vin II 139 [8, 99–100]. See also Gombrich's *What the Buddha Thought* [1, 146–48].

where the missions to Sri Lanka originated. A number of scholars are of the opinion that the West-Indian dialect associated with the Asokan rock edicts at Girnār and Bombay-Sopārā are closely related to Pali [7, 73–74] [9, 8–9]. The precise age of Pali, therefore, does not have any bearing on the age of the contents of the EBTs.

Finally, there are no certain traces of Sinhalese influence on the Pali EBTs [4, 246] [5, 102–103]. This suggests that the EBTs were in a standardised form when they arrived in Sri Lanka around the time of Asoka and that they are unlikely to have been changed after this. As Wynne says: "If the language of the Pali canon is north Indian in origin, and without substantial Sinhalese additions, it is likely that the canon was composed somewhere in north India before its introduction to Sri Lanka, and is therefore a source for the period of Buddhism in Northern India before this" [10], that is, before Asoka. In contrast, Pali texts actually composed in Sri Lanka do show influence from both Sinhalese and Dravidian [6, 6].

References

[1] GOMBRICH, Richard. *What the Buddha Thought*. Oxford Centre for Buddhist Studies monographs. Equinox, 2009.

[2] HINÜBER, Oskar VON. "Linguistic considerations on the date of the Buddha". In: *When Did the Buddha Live?: The Controversy on the Dating of the Historical Buddha*. Bibliotheca Indo-Buddhica. Sri Satguru, 1995.

[3] HINÜBER, Oskar VON. "Pali as an artificial language". In: *Indologica Taurinensa* 10 (1982). URL: http://www.indologica.com/volumes/vol10/vol10_art10_hinuber.pdf.

[4] NORMAN, K.R. *Collected Papers I*. The Pali Text Society, 1990.

[5] NORMAN, K.R. *Collected Papers VIII*. The Pali Text Society, 2007.

[6] NORMAN, K.R. *Pali Literature, Including the Canonical Literature in Prakrit and Sanskrit of all the Hinayana Schools of Buddhism*. Otto Harrassowitz, 1983.

[7] SALOMON, Richard. *Indian Epigraphy: A Guide to the Study of Inscriptions in Sanskrit, Prakrit, and the other Indo-Aryan Languages*. South Asia Research. Oxford University Press, USA, 1998.

[8] THANISSARO, Bhikkhu. *The Buddhist Monastic Code*. Vol. II. Thanissaro, Bhikkhu, 2002. URL: http://ebooks.gutenberg.us/WorldeBookLibrary.com/lib/modern/thanissaro/bmc2/ch08.html.

[9] WARDER, A.K. *Pali Metre*. The Pali Text Society, 1967.

[10] WYNNE, Alexander. *How old is the Suttapiṭaka? The relative value of textual and epigraphical sources for the study of early Indian Buddhism*. 2003. URL: http://www.budsas.org/ebud/ebsut056.htm.

3.6 Manuscripts

The earliest extant Indic manuscripts include EBTs and other Buddhist texts derived directly or indirectly from the EBTs.

The earliest Indian manuscripts are the Gāndhārī Buddhist texts from Afghanistan, the earliest of which date to the 1st century CE [4].[20] These contain a Dhammapada, discourses in verse (for example the Rhinoceros Sutta) and discourses in prose (including several Saṁyutta and Aṅguttara style texts), as well as non-EBT texts, such as Avadānas and Pūrvayogas, commentaries and Abhidharma texts.

This pattern of textual distribution conforms to that expected of the period immediately after the beginning of the common era. Many of the texts belong to the EBTs, and those that have been studied in detail show a close affinity with other EBTs.[21] The remainder of these texts are non-EBTs that form part of the textual development immediately based on the EBTs.

References

[1] BRAARVIG, Jens et al., eds. *Buddhist manuscripts of the Schøyen collection vol. I*. Hermes Academic Publishing, 2000. URL: http://www.hermesac.no/Prospect_Hermes_100806.pdf.

[2] FALK, Harry. "The "Split" Collection of Kharoṣṭhī Texts". In: *Annual Report of the International Research Institute for Advanced Buddhology at Soka University (ARIRIAB)*. Vol. XIV. 2011, pp. 13–24. URL: http://www.academia.edu/3561702/split_collection.

[20] Another early collection of Gāndhārī texts is The Schøyen Collection [1]. There are also other scattered early manuscripts, e.g. [2] [5].

[21] In his study of the the Gāndhārī fragments of the Senior collection, Andrew Glass says: "The traditions which eventually produced the Pali and Gāndhārī texts preserved much the same wording in their texts" and "The differences in the next three Sūtras from their parallels in the Saṁyutta Nikāya are in all cases minor." [3, 65, 63]

[3] GLASS, Andrew, trans. *Connected Discourses in Gandhāra*. PhD thesis. University of Washington, 2006.

[4] SALOMON, Richard. *Ancient Buddhist Scrolls from Gandhāra*. Gandharan Buddhist Texts. University of Washington Press, 1999. URL: http://www.ebmp.org/p_abt.php.

[5] STRAUCH, Ingo. *The Bajaur collection: A new collection of Kharoṣṭhī manuscripts. A preliminary catalogue and survey*. 2008. URL: http://www.geschkult.fu-berlin.de/e/indologie/bajaur/publication/strauch_2008_1_1.pdf?1347696630.

3.7 Scholarly opinion

There is a loose consensus among specialists in early Buddhism that the EBTs are in the main authentic.

Scholars thrive on disagreement. Nevertheless, among those who specialise in this field, there has been, since the beginnings of modern Buddhist studies, a rough working consensus that at least part of the EBTs are authentic. Academic sceptics of authenticity are almost always specialists in later Buddhism, making comments outside their own field. The following are some examples of the views of scholars of h Buddhism.

1. Rupert Gethin: "Far from representing sectarian Buddhism, these Suttas [the four main Nikāyas] above all constitute the common ancient heritage of Buddhism" [3, XXI] and "it is extremely likely that at least some of these Suttas that come down to us are among the oldest surviving Buddhist texts and contain material that goes back directly to the Buddha." [3, XVIII]

2. Richard Gombrich says "the content of the main body of sermons, the four Nikāyas and of the main body of monastic rules ... presents such originality, intelligence, grandeur and—most relevantly—coherence, that it is hard to see it as a composite work." They are "the work of one genius", the Buddha [4, 21].

3. Peter Harvey also affirms that "much" of the Pali Canon "must derive from his [the Buddha's] teachings." [5, 3]

4. J.W. de Jong has said it would be "hypocritical" to assert that we can say nothing about the teachings of earliest Buddhism, arguing that "the basic ideas of Buddhism found in the canonical writings could very well have been proclaimed by him [the Buddha], transmitted and developed by his disciples and, finally, codified in fixed formulas." [6, 25]

5. Lamotte says that "Buddhism could not be explained unless we accept that it has its origin in the strong personality of its founder." [7, 639]

6. Hajime Nakamura writes that while nothing can be definitively attributed to Gotama as a historical figure, some sayings or phrases must derive from him [10, 57].

7. Noble Ross Reat: "Though the Pali Suttas obviously exaggerate and mythologize the qualities and deeds of the Buddha, with regard to his teachings they have every appearance of constituting for the most part a faithful and reasonably accurate record." [11, 17]

8. A.K. Warder has stated that "there is no evidence to suggest that it [the shared teaching of the early schools] was formulated by anyone other than the Buddha and his immediate followers." [14, inside flap]

9. Maurice Winternitz: "Speeches... which again and again recur word for word in the same form not only in many places in the Pali canon but also in Buddhist Sanskrit texts... [and] Tibetan and Chinese translation, we may perhaps consider as originating from Buddha..." [15, 5]

10. Alexander Wynne: "I therefore agree with Rhys Davids, and disagree with sceptics such as Senart, Kern, and Schopen, that the internal evidence of the early Buddhist literature proves its historical authenticity." [16, 65]

Examples of critics of authenticity, who are specialists in later Buddhism, include:

1. Edward Conze states that the confident attempts of European scholars to reconstruct the original teachings of the Buddha himself are "all mere guesswork" [1, 9].

2. Ronald Davidson has little confidence that much, if any, of surviving Buddhist scripture is actually the word of the historical Buddha [2, 147].

3. Karen Lang suggests that there is no way of knowing how closely the Canon written down in the last century BCE resembles that of the present day [8].

4. Kogen Mizuno suggests that the Suttas as we possess them may not contain the Buddha's literal words, since they were not recorded as he spoke [9, 22].

5. Geoffrey Samuel says the Pali Canon largely derives from the work of Buddhaghosa and his colleagues in the 5th century CE [12, 48].

6. Gregory Schopen argues that it is not until the 5th to 6th centuries CE that we can know anything definite about the contents of the Canon [13, 24].

References

[1] CONZE, Edward. *Buddhism: A Short History.* From Buddhism to Sufism Series. Oneworld, 2000.

[2] DAVIDSON, R.M. *Indian Esoteric Buddhism: Social History of the Tantric Movement.* Motilal Banarsidass, 2004.

[3] GETHIN, Rupert, trans. *Sayings of the Buddha: New Translations from the Pali Nikayas.* Oxford World's Classics. Oxford University Press, 2008.

[4] GOMBRICH, Richard. *Theravāda Buddhism: A Social History from Ancient Benares to Modern Colombo.* The Library of Religious Beliefs and Practices Series. Routledge & Kegan Paul, 2006.

[5] HARVEY, Peter. *An Introduction to Buddhism: Teachings, History and Practices.* Introduction to Religion. Cambridge University Press, 1990.

[6] JONG, J.W. de. "The Beginnings of Buddhism". In: *The Eastern Buddhist* 26 (1993), pp. 35–70.

[7] LAMOTTE, Étienne. *History of Indian Buddhism: From the Origins to the Śaka Era.* Publications de l'Institut orientaliste de Louvain. Université catholique de Louvain, Institut orientaliste, 1988.

[8] LANG, Karen. "Pali Canon". In: *The Encyclopedia of Buddhism.* Routledge, 2007.

[9] MIZUNO, Kogen. *Buddhist Sutras: Origin, Development, Transmission.* Kosei, 1982.

[10] NAKAMURA, Hajime. *Indian Buddhism: a survey with bibliographical notes.* Intercultural Research Institute monograph series. KUFS Publication, 1980.

[11] REAT, Noble Ross. "The Historical Buddha and his Teachings". In: *Encyclopedia of Indian Philosophy.* Ed. by POTTER, Karl H. Vol. VII: Abhidharma Buddhism to 150 AD. Motilal Banarsidass, 1996, pp. 3–57.

[12] SAMUEL, G. *Introducing Tibetan Buddhism.* World Religions Series. Routledge, 2012.

[13] SCHOPEN, Gregory. *Bones, Stones, and Buddhist Monks.* University of Hawai'i Press, 1997.

[14] WARDER, A.K. *Indian Buddhism.* Buddhism Series. Motilal Banarsidass, 2000.

[15] WINTERNITZ, M. *A History of Indian Literature.* History of Indian Literature. Motilal Banarsidass, 1983. URL: `http://www.scribd.com/doc/61244543/Maurice-Winternitz-History-of-Indian-Literature-Vol-II-1933`.

[16] WYNNE, Alexander. "The Historical Authenticity of Early Buddhist Literature". In: *Vienna Journal of South Asian Studies* XLIX (2005), pp. 35–70. URL: `http://www.ocbs.org/images/stories/awynne2005wzks.pdf`.

3.8 Stability of consensus

The mostly recent views of the scholars cited above largely confirm the conclusions of the early generation of Indologists.

We cannot hope to represent the wide range of scholarly views over the past 100–150 years. Instead, we selectively quote some of the most distinguished early scholars in the field, and in the process hope to present a reasonable range of views of 19th century Indologists, showing that these tend to affirm the authenticity of the EBTS.

1. In 1882 Samuel Beal stated that the texts of the various schools were "founded on one and the same traditional record" [1, 48].

2. Beal said in 1884 that the *pātimokkha* "is the oldest, and in many respects the most important, material of the vinaya literature." [2, 23] This position was the same as that taken by Rhys Davids and Oldenberg in 1879 [5, introduction].

3. Beal: "It is clear they [the Mahāyāna texts, specifically the Prajñā Pāramitā] cannot belong to the early school or have formed a part of the original collection of books." [2, 38]

4. Dr. Hofrath Bühler said that the Pali Nikāyas are good evidence for the fifth or sixth century BCE [8, XXI].

5. Wilhelm Geiger: "But without a doubt it [the canon] contains a mass of utterances, speeches and teachings of the Master, as they were impressed on the memory of the disciples in their more or less accurate form." [3, 12]

6. Oldenberg argued that the *pātimokkha* and the "fundamental doctrines of the Dhamma" were from the same period, whereas the rest of the Vinaya was later [5, XXIV], and that the Abhidhamma was later than the Sutta and the Vinaya Piṭakas [5, X–XIII].

7. Oldenberg maintained that all "versions of the vinaya are based upon one foundation" [5, XLVII], and said: "Hence our opinion of the early origin of the Buddhist texts [the EBTs], based as it is on external proofs, does not clash, but agrees with the internal possibility and probability." [5, XXXIX–XL]

8. Pachow, referring principally to Oldenberg and Kern, says: "It has been admitted by all eminent scholars that the Pmk [Prātimokṣa] is one of the oldest texts of the Buddhist Canon." [6, 14] E.J. Thomas agrees [10, 161–166].

9. T.W. Rhys Davids: "Their composition, as to the Vinaya and the four Nikāyas (with the possible exception of the supplements),[22] was complete within about a century of the Buddha's death." [9, v]

10. T.W. Rhys Davids, referring to inscriptions on ancient stupas that mention *suttantika, suttantakinī, pañcanekāyika, dhammakathika*, and *peṭakī*, says these terms constitute "conclusive proof of the existence some considerable time before the date of the inscriptions, of a Buddhist literature called either a Piṭaka or the Piṭakas, containing suttantas, and divided into Five Nikāyas." [8, xi]

Having reviewed the conclusions of some of the most noted scholars, it seems clear that, despite difference in details, many of the basic insights of the first generation of 19th century Indologists remain valid. This is despite the notable advances and changes in understanding due to expanded sources and clearer analysis. The situation is comparable to that in biology. Just as the insights of Darwin, though often refined and modified, still provide the framework for modern biology, so this rough consensus extends beyond these general statements and provides the framework within which modern Buddhist scholars continue to work.

Finally, let us look at the more specific findings of one of the most noted pioneers of Buddhist studies. Here is a chronology of Pali Buddhist texts from T.W. Rhys Davids in the appendix to chapter 10 of *Buddhist India* [7, 188].

Chronological table of Buddhist literature from the Buddha's time to the time of Asoka

1. The simple statements of Buddhist doctrine now found, in identical words, in paragraphs or verses recurring in all the books.

2. Episodes found, in identical words, in two or more of the existing books.

3. The Sīlas, the Pārāyana, the Octades, the *pātimokkha*.

[22] It is not entirely clear what "supplements" refers to, but most likely it is the Khuddaka Nikāya, or at least parts thereof, and the Parivāra of the Vinaya Piṭaka.

4. The Dīgha, Majjhima, Aṅguttara, and Saṁyutta Nikāyas.
5. The Sutta Nipāta, the Thera- and Therī-Gāthās, the Udānas, and the Khuddaka Pāṭha.
6. The Sutta Vibhaṅga and the Khandhakas.
7. The Jātakas and the Dhammapadas.
8. The Niddesa, the Itivuttakas, and the Paṭisambhidā.
9. The Peta- and Vimāna-Vatthus, the Apadānas, the Cariyā Piṭaka, and the Buddha Vaṁsa.
10. The Abhidhamma books; the last of which is the Kathā Vatthu, and the earliest probably the Puggala Paññatti.

This is obviously meant as a simple aid to orientation among the material, not as definitive or exhaustive. In an excellent example of the friendly and critical debates that characterised this period of early Indology, the list was swiftly criticised and nuanced by Bimala Law [4, ch. 1]. Nevertheless, if we allow for the limitations of such a simple presentation of such a complex subject, his sequence holds up very well. The main changes we would suggest is to place the Itivuttaka with the Udāna and other texts at number 5, and to allow that the Abhidhamma was compiled alongside the other texts, probably from number 6 on, or at least from number 8.

References

[1] BEAL, Samuel. *Abstract of Four Lectures On Buddhist Literature in China*. BiblioLife, 2010. URL: http://archive.org/details/cu31924023158607.

[2] BEAL, Samuel. *Buddhism in China*. Society for Promoting Christian Knowledge, 1884. URL: http://archive.org/details/buddhisminchina00commgoog.

[3] GEIGER, W. and GHOSH, B. *Pāli literature and language*. University of Calcutta, 1943.

[4] LAW, B.C. *A History of Pali Literature*. Kegan Paul, Trench, Trubner, & Co., 1933. ISBN: 9780879685355.

[5] OLDENBERG, H., ed. *Vinaya Piṭaka*. Pali Text Society, 1879–1883.

[6] PACHOW, W. *A Comparative Study of the Pratimoksha: On the Basis of its Chinese, Tibetan, Sanskrit and Pali Versions*. Motilal Banarsidass, 2000.

[7] RHYS DAVIDS, T.W. *Buddhist India*. Putnam, 1903. URL: http://fsnow.com/text/buddhist-india/.

[8] RHYS DAVIDS, T.W., trans. *Dialogues of the Buddha*. Vol. I. Dialogues of the Buddha: Translated from the Pali of the Dīgha Nikāya. Motilal Banarsidass, 2000.

[9] RHYS DAVIDS, T.W. and STEDE, W. *The Pali-English Dictionary*. Asian Educational Services, 2004.

[10] THOMAS, E.J. "Pre-Pāli terms in the Pātimokkha". In: *Festschrift Moriz Winternitz*. Otto Harrassowitz, 1933, pp. 161–166.

CHAPTER 4

Character of the Early Buddhist Texts

The simplest explanation for the unique character of the EBTs is that they stem, in the main, from a single author, the historical Buddha.

Most of the EBTs state explicitly that the Buddha is their author. The character of the EBTs is most easily accounted for if this is, on the whole, true. There are obvious exceptions, such as where the speaker is specifically said to be someone else, or where there are indications that texts or passages have been added. These exceptions, however, should not be allowed to distract from the overall picture.[1]

The EBTs are stylistically different from other Buddhist texts, as well as internally consistent in both doctrine and phrasing. They are a separate genre of literature [2, 113]. This is most simply explained if they hark back to a common source in the earliest period. They have a different authorship from other Buddhist texts, and are the root texts from which the rest of Buddhist literary activity developed.

References

[1] GOMBRICH, Richard. *What the Buddha Thought*. Oxford Centre for Buddhist Studies monographs. Equinox, 2009.

1 Gombrich says: "But our initial working hypothesis has to be that the text is telling the truth, and in each case where we do not believe it, or doubt it, we must produce our reasons for doing so." [1, 96–97]

[2] WYNNE, Alexander. "The Oral Transmission of the Early Buddhist Literature". In: *Journal of the International Association of Buddhist Studies* 27.1 (2004), pp. 97–127. URL: http://archiv.ub.uni-heidelberg.de/ojs/index.php/jiabs/article/view/8945/2838.

4.1 Vedic influence on the EBTs

The literary form of the EBTs is strongly influenced by the Brahmanical Vedas, which shows that they are the first generation of Buddhist literature, emerging in a non-Buddhist context.

The EBTs frequently bear the stamp of influence from Brahmanical literature in their literary style. The most obvious is the poetry, where we find that the metres are developed from Vedic precedent [6, 15–16].[2] Likewise, the characteristic feature of framing narratives is derived from the Vedas [5]. In the Vedas we also find the models for such organising principles as the Saṁyutta principle of grouping texts by topic,[3] and the Aṅguttara principle of grouping them according to number [2, 23–24] [3, 101]. The EBTs frequently share metaphors and imagery with the Vedic literature. Indeed, we can point to several shared similes in just one Upaniṣadic passage, the dialogue between Yājñavalkya and his wife Maitreyī: the origin of the sound of the conch or the lute, (DN 23.19/DĀ 7/MĀ 71/T 45 vs. Bṛhadāraṇyaka Upaniṣad 2.4.7–9), the rivers that merge in the ocean (AN 8:19 vs. Bṛhadāraṇyaka Upaniṣad 2.4.11), and the ocean that everywhere has one taste, the taste of salt (AN 8.157 vs. Bṛhadāraṇyaka Upaniṣad 2.4.11). Finally, the EBTs borrowed a significant number of Brahmanical terms and ideas, often infusing them with a new meaning [3, 28, 43–44, 80–81, 122–128, 133–137, 182, 188, 202–206]. All of these ideas and forms were invariably adapted to a Buddhist use.

This shows that the EBTs adopted aspects of the Brahmanical model, which at that time was the only available example of a successful and lasting literary tradition. This is despite the enormous differences between

[2] Warder says: "The Pali *vatta* [metre] is close in structure to that of the Brāhmaṇas and early Upaniṣads, and apparently a little later in date ..."

[3] The Ṛg Veda, for instance, is organised according to the names of the gods, similar to the organising principle of the Sagāthā Vagga of the Saṁyutta Nikāya. See also [4, 196].

the EBTs and the Vedas [3, 165].[4] All other forms of Buddhist texts, by contrast, are derived primarily from earlier forms of Buddhist literature.

References

[1] BRONKHORST, Johannes. *Greater Magadha: studies in the culture of early India.* Brill, 2007.

[2] GOMBRICH, Richard. "How the Mahayana Began". In: *Buddhist Forum* I (2012), pp. 21–30. URL: http://www.shin-ibs.edu/documents/bForum/v1/01Gombrich.pdf.

[3] GOMBRICH, Richard. *What the Buddha Thought.* Oxford Centre for Buddhist Studies monographs. Equinox, 2009.

[4] HINÜBER, Oskar VON. "Hoary past and hazy memory. On the history of early Buddhist texts". In: *Journal of the International Association of Buddhist Studies* 29.2 (2006), pp. 193–210.

[5] SUJATO, Bhikkhu. *Concerning baskets.* 26 December 2012. URL: http://sujato.wordpress.com/2012/12/26/concerning-baskets/.

[6] WARDER, A.K. *Pali Metre.* The Pali Text Society, 1967.

4.2 Literary features

Analysis of linguistic style reveals a specific set of characteristics that is unique to the EBTs and not shared with non-EBT literature.

In his book *Buddhist India*, T.W. Rhys Davids says:

> "On the other hand, suppose a MS. were discovered containing, in the same handwriting, copies of Bacon's Essays and of Hume's Essay, with nothing to show when, or by whom, they were written; and that we knew nothing at all otherwise about the matter. Still we should know, with absolute certainty, which was relatively the older of the two; and should be able to determine, within a quite short period, the actual date of each of the two works. The evidence would

[4] Bronkhorst says [1, 255]: "This feature is perhaps difficult to pin down exactly, but becomes clear to most readers who read a passage from a late-Vedic text and one, say, from a Buddhist sermon side by side. The way of thinking one is confronted with in the former is very different—more 'primitive'—than that in the latter."

be irresistible because it would consist of a very large number of minute points of language, of style, and, above all, of ideas expressed, all tending in the same direction.

"This is the sort of internal evidence that we have before us in the Pali books. Any one who habitually reads Pali would know at once that the Nikāyas are older than the Dhamma Saṅgaṇi; that both are older than the Kathā Vatthu; that all three are older than the Milinda. And the Pali scholars most competent to judge are quite unanimous on the point, and on the general position of the Pali literature in the history of literature in India.

"But this sort of evidence can appeal, of course, only to those familiar with the language and with the ideas." [1, ch. 10]

We will now have a look at some of the stylistic features that make the EBTs stand apart from other Buddhist texts.

References

[1] RHYS DAVIDS, T.W. *Buddhist India*. Putnam, 1903. URL: http://fsnow.com/text/buddhist-india/.

4.2.1 Grammar

The Pali EBTs have grammatical features of Western India, and even of Magadha, but not of Sri Lanka.

The geographical distribution of language features for the time shortly after the Buddha is known primarily from the Asokan edicts [4, 155]. It is generally accepted that Pali has its roots in Western India in the region of Avanti [1, 181–183] [5, 103], which is on the trade route to Sri Lanka.

At the same time, it has been shown that the vocabulary of the Pali EBTs preserves several early dialectical forms (Magadhisms)[5] that are generally regarded as linguistic remnants from the time when Buddhism was geographically limited to the Eastern part of India [1, 182–183] [5, 105, 110–111].

[5] E.g. masculine a-stem nominative singulars in 'e' [3, 46–47], masculine a-stem nominative plurals in 'āse' [5, 111], l's occurring where one would normally expect r's [3, 47], and a number of other features [3, 47–48].

These features are not found in other Buddhist literature, with the exception of the Kathāvatthu, which may have these forms due to its probable origin in Magadha [2, 65, 69].

References

[1] HINÜBER, Oskar VON. *Selected papers on Pali studies.* The Pali Text Society, 1994.

[2] NORMAN, K.R. *Collected Papers II.* The Pali Text Society, 1991.

[3] NORMAN, K.R. *Collected Papers IV.* The Pali Text Society, 1993.

[4] NORMAN, K.R. *Collected Papers V.* The Pali Text Society, 1994.

[5] NORMAN, K.R. *Collected Papers VIII.* The Pali Text Society, 2007.

4.2.2 Vocabulary

The vocabulary of the EBTs is derived from the Upaniṣads and other contemporary sources, while the non-EBTs derive theirs from the EBTs and later trends.

The vocabulary of the EBTs is different from that of other Buddhist texts. The easiest way to see this difference is to compare passages in the EBTs with parallel passages in other Buddhist literature. Such comparison suggests that the other texts belong to a later chronological stratum than the EBTs. There are countless examples of this, one of which is the standard formula for *satipaṭṭhāna* as found in the EBTs compared with that found in the Vibhaṅga of the Abhidhamma.

1. The standard *satipaṭṭhāna* formula of the Suttas is as follows (e.g. MN 10.3):

   Idha, bhikkhave, bhikkhu kāye kāyānupassī viharati ātāpī sampajāno satimā, vineyya loke abhijjhādomanassaṁ.

2. The *satipaṭṭhāna* formula of the *Suttanta-bhājanīya* ("Sutta analysis") of the Vibhaṅga is as follows (Vibh 193,1):

   idha bhikkhu ajjhattaṁ kāye kāyānupassī viharati bahiddhā kāye kāyānupassī viharati ajjhattabahiddhā kāye kāyānupassī viharati ātāpī sampajāno satimā vineyya loke abhijjhādomanassaṁ.

3. And the *satipaṭṭhāna* formula of the *Abhidhamma-bhājanīya* ("Abhidhamma analysis") of the Vibhaṅga is as follows (Vibh 203,1):

   Idha bhikkhu yasmiṁ samaye lokuttaraṁ jhānaṁ bhāveti niyyānikaṁ apacayagāmiṁ diṭṭhigatānaṁ pahānāya paṭhamāya bhūmiyā pattiyā vivicceva kāmehi ...pe... paṭhamaṁ jhānaṁ upasampajja viharati dukkhapaṭipadaṁ dandhābhiññaṁ kāye kāyānupassī, yā tasmiṁ samaye sati anussati sammāsati satisambojjhaṅgo maggaṅgaṁ maggapariyāpannaṁ—idaṁ vuccati "satipaṭṭhānaṁ". Avasesā dhammā satipaṭṭhānasampayuttā.

The first formula is the standard Sutta formula, whereas the second one constitutes the earliest development of the Abhidhammma.[6] It is only at the third stage that we find the formula in fully fledged Abhidhamma style.

The formula in stage 2 is virtually identical with the Sutta formula, and in fact the formula is found in this form in some non-Pali EBTS.[7] This close relationship is to be expected since this constitutes an analysis according to the Suttas. Yet further on in the same Sutta analysis typical Abhidhamma vocabulary, such as *svāvatthitaṁ* and *vavatthāpeti*, is introduced (Vibh. 193,24). We seem to be witnessing the beginning of the Abhidhamma method.

At stage 3 we have the analysis according to the Abhidhamma. Here the whole *satipaṭṭhāna* formula is completely transformed and we see a range of vocabulary that is either unknown to the EBTS or used in a new sense: *yasmiṁ samaye*, *lokuttaraṁ jhānaṁ*, *paṭhamāya bhūmiyā*, *avasesā dhammā satipaṭṭhānasampayuttā*, and so on.

This is just one example of a pattern that plays out, not just here, but in every major doctrinal context or formula.

References

[1] FRAUWALLNER, E., KIDD, S.F., and STEINKELLNER, E. *Studies in Abhidharma Literature and the Origins of Buddhist Philosophical Systems*. SUNY Series in Indian Thought. State University of New York Press, 1995.

6 These kinds of formula constitute the common core of the different recensions of the Abhidhamma, which therefore must go back to the pre-sectarian era [1, 19–20], See section 6.4.2, "Early Abhidhamma".

7 E.g. SMPS 10.14.

4.2.3 Metre

By analysing the history of Indian metre it is possible to locate verses in history and thereby help identify the EBTs.

Metre—the rhythmic structure of verse—is constantly changing, and thus it is possible to identify the type of metre popular for any particular historical period. By careful metric analysis, it is possible to arrive at the approximate period in which a particular poem must have been composed.

It is sometimes suggested that certain verses found in the EBTs are particularly ancient due to archaic words and grammatical features [1, 27]. However, according to the late A.K. Warder, perhaps the world's leading authority on Pali verse, archaic word forms in verse often are deliberate rather than showing the true chronological stratum to which the text belongs [2, 10]. Metrical analysis gets us around this problem and promises a more direct relative dating of Pali verse.

One of the earliest forms of the Pali metre, known as *vatta*, is close in structure to the *vatta* metre as used in the Upaniṣads, but chronologically slightly later. However, the same metre is earlier than that of the Bṛhaddevatā and still earlier than that of the Mahābhārata [2, 16].

According to Warder, "It seems certain that the verse parts of the Pali Canon represent quite a long period of composition" [2, 212], and that "The differences of age thus suggested seem to agree with the general drift of subjective opinion on which sort of doctrine is earlier and which later." [2, 197] But he also says that, "Although we cannot say whether any Pali verses in their present form date back to the time of the Buddha (i.e. circa 500 BCE), on the one hand the changes in techniques within the Canon imply a considerable period of development prior to the 2nd century BCE, and on the other hand the formal similarities between the Canon and those of the other early schools indicate a common origin of the original 'kernels' in a period before the sectarian divisions had separated them too far." [2, 6]

Within the Pali canon, the metrically oldest verses are found in the Aṭṭhaka Vagga and the Pārāyana Vagga of the Sutta Nipāta [2, 16]. Metrical analysis also shows that the Pārāyana Vagga can be further divided into a core of very ancient poems and the surrounding narrative framework [2, 199]. This fits with our general observation, and also with the results of comparative study, that the narratives are later than the actual words attributed to the Buddha.

References

[1] NAKAMURA, Hajime. *Indian Buddhism: a survey with bibliographical notes.* Intercultural Research Institute monograph series. KUFS Publication, 1980.

[2] WARDER, A.K. *Pali Metre.* The Pali Text Society, 1967.

4.2.4 Style

> *The EBTs tend to be straight to the point and realistic, whereas non-EBTs are often highly embellished and full of supernatural events.*

The EBTs are generally realistic and restrained in their portrayal of the Buddha and his environment, and the details do not seem unreasonable for what we know of the historical period and geographical area. For instance, the Buddha is rarely portrayed as displaying supernormal powers, and when he is they often have the hallmarks of being later insertions.[8]

Non-EBTs, by contrast, are often florid and full of supernormal phenomena. This is true for the entire Buddhist tradition, but especially so for the Mahāyāna Sūtras. The Mahāyāna Sūtras generally lack the realism of the EBTs [4, 199] [5, 49].

This difference can be appreciated by considering the opening narrative of a typical text in the Majjhima Nikāya compared to the opening of a classical Mahāyāna text from the Prajñā-pāramitā corpus. A typical Sutta in the Majjhima Nikāya starts as follows:

> "Thus have I heard. On one occasion the Blessed One was living at Sāvatthī in Jeta's Grove, Anāthapiṇḍika's Park. There he addressed the bhikkhus thus: ..."

A short extract (about 10%) of the opening of the the Large Prajñā-pāramitā Sūtra, according to Conze's translation [3, 37–39], reads as follows:

[8] This can be seen through comparative study, where supernormal powers mentioned in one recension of a Sutta often do not appear in its parallels. For one example of this see [2, note 452]; see also [1, note 34]

> "Thus have I heard. At one time the Lord dwelt at Rājagṛha, on the Vulture Peak, together with a large gathering of monks, with 1,250 monks, all of them Arhats—their outflows dried up, undefiled, fully controlled, quite freed in their hearts, well freed and wise, thoroughbreds, great Serpents, their work done, their task accomplished, their burden laid down, their own weal accomplished, with the fetters that bound them to becoming extinguished, their hearts well freed by right understanding, in perfect control of their whole minds—with 500 nuns, laymen, and laywomen, all of them liberated in this present life—and with hundreds of thousands of *niyutas* of *koṭis* of Bodhisattvas.[9] ... Thereupon the Lord on that occasion put out his tongue. With it he covered the great trichiliocosm and many hundreds of thousands of *niyutas* of *koṭis* of rays issued from it. From each one of these rays there arose lotuses, made of the finest precious stones, of golden colour, and with thousands of petals; and on those lotuses there were, seated and standing, Buddha-frames demonstrating dharma, i.e. this very demonstration of dharma associated with the six perfections. They went in all the ten directions to countless world systems in each direction, and demonstrated dharma to beings, i.e. this very demonstration of dharma associated with the six perfections. And the beings who heard this demonstration of dharma, they became fixed on the utmost, right and perfect enlightenment."

This is an entirely different kind of literature, one which is completely uninterested in history; so much so that it flaunts its creativity. The purpose of the introduction is no longer to identify time and place, but to lift the reader out of history to a timeless realm of Dharma.

Differences in style manifest in other ways too. Rhys Davids comments as follows on the stylistic difference between earlier and later works in the Theravāda tradition:

> "The philosophic ideas of the ancient Buddhism, and the psychological ideas on which they were based, were often curtly, naively, confusedly expressed. In Ceylon they had been much worked up, polished, elucidated, systematised. From several works now accessible we know fairly well the tone and manner of these later—and,

[9] That is, trillions of Bodhisattvas.

as they must have seemed to Ceylon scholars, clearer, fuller—statements of the old ideas. In no single instance yet discovered has this later tone and manner found its way into the canonical books ." [6, ch. 10]

References

[1] ANĀLAYO. "The Chinese Parallels to the Dhammacakkappavattana-sutta (2)". In: *Journal of the Oxford Centre for Buddhist Studies* 5 (2013), pp. 9–41.

[2] BODHI, Bhikkhu, trans. *The Numerical Discourses of the Buddha: A Translation of the Aṅguttara Nikāya*. Teachings of the Buddha. Wisdom Publications, 2012.

[3] CONZE, Edward, trans. *The Large Sutra on Perfect Wisdom*. University of California Press, 1975. URL: http://lirs.ru/lib/conze/The_Large_Sutra_On_Perfect_Wisdom,Conze,1975.pdf.

[4] GOMBRICH, Richard. *What the Buddha Thought*. Oxford Centre for Buddhist Studies monographs. Equinox, 2009.

[5] MCMAHAN, David. "Orality, Writing, and Authority in South Asian Buddhism: Visionary Literature and the Struggle for Legitimacy in the Mahāyāna". In: *History of Religions* 37 (1998), pp. 249–274. URL: http://ccbs.ntu.edu.tw/FULLTEXT/JR-EPT/mc.htm.

[6] RHYS DAVIDS, T.W. *Buddhist India*. Putnam, 1903. URL: http://fsnow.com/text/buddhist-india/.

4.2.5 Oral vs. literary tradition

The EBTs are an oral literature, and must have been fully composed long before the use of writing for sacred literature (no later than the first century BCE).

The EBTs depict the Buddha as being concerned about the long-term preservation of his message (DN 16.3.50/SMPS 19.7, DN 29.17), as saying that the EBTs would preserve the Dhamma (DN 16.3.50/SMPS 19.8–9),[10] and

[10] "Monks, for this reason those matters which I have discovered and proclaimed should be thoroughly learnt by you, practised, developed and cultivated, so that this holy life may endure for a long time ... They are: The four foundations of mindfulness, the four right efforts, the four roads to power, the five spiritual faculties, the five mental powers the seven factors of enlightenment, the Noble Eightfold Path." We are thus equating the *bodhipakkhiya dhammas* with the EBTs. The Buddha often speaks of these teachings as being the core of his message, e.g. at MN 103.3–8 and MN 104.5.

as giving guidance and encouragement on how to do this (DN 16.4.7–11/ SMPS 24.2–52, MN 103.4–8). The mnemonic features of the EBTs (see section 3.2 above) serve precisely the purpose of ensuring the long-term reliable transmission of the texts.

These features are not incidental or added on, they are intrinsic to the EBTs. Let us consider one of these features, repetition. If repetition was a conscious device used by later redactors to ensure fidelity, but not part of the Buddha's style, we would expect to find repetition only in those aspects of the texts that the redactors controlled. For example, we would find the same Sutta repeated in multiple collections. However, what we actually find is that repetition is prevalent at every level of the texts, whether the word, the phrase, the sentence, the paragraph, the passage, or the whole discourse. Repetition, like the other mnemonic features of the texts, is a characteristic of their composition, a characteristic that was further developed by the redactors. Since the EBTs were composed in the oral tradition, the mnemonic characteristics of the texts originated in the historical Buddha's teaching style.

Most non-EBTs do not have such mnemonic features. This suggests that these texts were composed specifically for written rather than oral transmission. This would have been some time after the EBTs, when writing was in common use for Buddhist texts.[11]

The exception to this is the later strata of canonical material, such as the Abhidhamma, much of the Vinaya, and some of the Suttas, especially in the Khuddaka Nikāya, but also some of the material in the main Nikāyas/Āgamas. This material retains the features of the oral tradition, yet on multiple other grounds it is clearly later than the EBTs. It would, of course, have taken considerable time for the literary style to emerge fully from the oral culture, just as the earliest builders in stone for a long time employed principles of wood work, or just as digital designers now employ skeuomorphism. Even the Mahāyāna Sūtras, which were composed in writing and which frequently refer to writing [1] [2, 251, 255, 257], retain some oral features such as repetition [2, 273]. This shows that the oral tradition

[11] The two most commonly cited references to the systematic writing down of Buddhist texts are found at Dīpavaṁsa 20.20–20.21 and Mahāvaṁsa 33.100–33.101, which date this to the first century BCE. However, it is quite conceivable that the practice, whether on a small or a large scale, may have started before then.

was firmly established and must have flourished for a considerable period before the texts were put in writing.

References

[1] GOMBRICH, Richard. “How the Mahayana Began”. In: *Buddhist Forum* I (2012), pp. 21–30. URL: http://www.shin-ibs.edu/documents/bForum/v1/01Gombrich.pdf.

[2] MCMAHAN, David. “Orality, Writing, and Authority in South Asian Buddhism: Visionary Literature and the Struggle for Legitimacy in the Mahāyāna”. In: *History of Religions* 37 (1998), pp. 249–274. URL: http://ccbs.ntu.edu.tw/FULLTEXT/JR-EPT/mc.htm.

4.3 Flavour of a single creator

The EBTs present a highly distinctive personal style, together with a number of revolutionary ideas, which conveys the flavour of a single and exceptional creator.

This can be seen in a number of aspects of the EBTs, such as the large number of similes, analogies and metaphors that are vivid, precise in application, realistic and local, and formal in presentation [3, 6–7]; the analytical approach to language, which was unknown before the Buddha; use of irony and humour [2, 180–192]; and internal consistency and coherence [1, 21]. Moreover, many of the ideas presented in the EBTs are revolutionary for the time. This distinctive personal style is quite different from anything found in other Buddhist literature, or even in the Upaniṣads.

References

[1] GOMBRICH, Richard. *Theravāda Buddhism: A Social History from Ancient Benares to Modern Colombo*. The Library of Religious Beliefs and Practices Series. Routledge & Kegan Paul, 2006.

[2] GOMBRICH, Richard. *What the Buddha Thought*. Oxford Centre for Buddhist Studies monographs. Equinox, 2009.

[3] HECKER, Helmut. *Similes of the Buddha*. Buddhist Publication Society, 2009.

4.3.1 Consistency and coherence

The EBTs are coherent and consistent—more so than any comparable literature—which indicates that they stem from a single charismatic source.

The EBTs are characterised by a rigorous consistency in doctrinal teachings [1, 17], together with a great variety in themes, contexts, settings and presentations. Whether there are any significant doctrinal contradictions is doubtful, and in any case there are far less than in any comparable ancient literature.

It is not easy to quantify this, but comparison with the contemporary hegemonic literature, the Upaniṣads, is instructive. Though the Upaniṣads compass a much smaller quantity of texts, they have far more diversity and contradiction in doctrines. Choosing two topics at random, here is a comparison between the EBTs and the earliest and largest Upaniṣad, the Bṛhadāraṇyaka. We believe that a more detailed study along similar lines would show that this kind of difference is systemic.[12]

1. **Creation:** The EBTs consistently assert that it is not possible to know a first point (*agga*) of creation.[13] In the discourse "On Knowledge of Beginnings" (DN 27/DĀ 5/T 10/MĀ 154/EĀ 40.1) the Buddha starts his creation myth by saying, "There comes a time when the world ends ...". In the Bṛhadāraṇyaka there are six creation myths, which say that in the beginning there was either nothing (1.2.1), self (1.4.1, 1.4.17), Brahmā (1.4.10, 1.4.11), or water (5.5.1) [2].

2. **Senses:** The EBTs always list six senses (the regular five plus the mind) in the same sequence, and they never mix the senses with other things. The Bṛhadāraṇyaka offers no less than thirteen different lists of the senses, usually mixed with such things as breath and

[12] This does not prove that the Upaniṣads are philosophically inconsistent, merely that the details are.

[13] SN 15, SĀ 937–943, SĀ 945–950, SĀ 952, SĀ 954, SĀ 956, SĀ² 330–336, SĀ² 338–343, SĀ² 345, SĀ² 347–348, SĀ² 350, SĀ³ 11, EĀ 51.1–2, EĀ 52.3–4, EĀ² 30.

voice. They almost always vary in both the contents of the list and the sequence.[14]

References

[1] GOMBRICH, Richard. *What the Buddha Thought*. Oxford Centre for Buddhist Studies monographs. Equinox, 2009.

[2] RADHAKRISHNAN, S., trans. *The principal Upaniṣads*. Muirhead library of philosophy. Allen & Unwin, 1953. URL: http://books.google.com.au/books?id=IxEPAQAAIAAJ.

4.3.2 Internal cross-references

EBTs refer to other EBTs, but never to other Buddhist texts, which shows that they are an integrated whole.

The EBTs frequently refer to doctrinal categories, verses, similes, specific teachings, and even to full discourses found elsewhere in the EBTs. When such references are made, the meaning is only transparent for someone who knows the passage referred to. Moreover, although there is extensive internal cross-referencing of this kind, there are no references to other Buddhist texts.

This shows that throughout Buddhist history, the EBTs have been regarded as a separate genre of texts, and that they were seen as an integrated body of teachings that constituted the Buddha's message. Other Buddhist texts, by contrast, refer both to the EBTs and other texts.[15]

The amount of internal cross-referencing in the EBTs is truly staggering and only a thorough computer analysis might be able to uncover the full extent of it. Here we can only hope to give a taste of its extent:

1. **Named Sutta collections:** Aṭṭhaka Vagga (Snp ch. 4, cited at SN 22:3 and Vin I 196,36[16]); Pārāyana Vagga (Snp ch. 5, cited at SN 12:31, AN 3:32, AN 3:33, AN 4:41, AN 6:61, AN 7:53).

---

[14] See Bṛhadāraṇyaka sections 1.3, 1.5.21, 2.4.11, 2.4.14, 3.2.2–9, 3.4.2 (this recurs at 3.8.11 and elsewhere), 3.7.10, 3.8.8, 4.1.2–7, 4.13.24–31, 4.4.2 = 4.5.16, 6.1.8 [2]. Even when the same dialogue is repeated, the list of senses varies: 2.4.11, 4.5.12.

[15] The commentaries, for instance, refer to the EBTs, the Abhidhamma, the Visuddhimagga, etc.

[16] Significantly, this reference is found in all extant Vinayas [1, 860, note 29].

2. **Named Suttas:** Ajitapañha/Ajitamāṇavapucchā (Snp 5:1, cited at SN 22:31); Brahmajāla (DN 1/DĀ 21/T 21/P 1021, cited at SN 41:3); Dhammacakka (SN 56:11/SĀ 379/T 109/T 110/EĀ 19.2/P 747/P 1003, cited at SN 8:7, MN 141.2, MN 26.25/MĀ 204, AN 5:133, AN 4:118, AN 3:14); Kumāripañha (SN 4:25/SĀ 1092/SĀ² 31, cited at AN 10:26); Mahāpañha (AN 10:27/EĀ 46.8, cited at AN 10:28 and SN 41:8); Māgaṇḍiyapañha (Snp 4:9, cited at SN 22:3); Metteyyapañha/Tissametteyyamāṇavapucchā (Snp 5:2, cited at AN 6:61); Pañcālacaṇḍa (SN 2:7/SĀ 1305/SĀ² 304, cited at AN 9:42); Puṇṇakapañha/Puṇṇakamāṇavapucchā (Snp 5:3, cited at AN 3:32 and AN 4:41); Sakkapañha (DN 21/DĀ 14/T 15/MĀ 134, cited at SN 22:4); Udayapañha/Udayamāṇavapucchā (Snp 5:13, cited at AN 3:33).

3. **Named doctrinal categories:**[17] four noble truths (DN 9.33, MN 77.14/MĀ 207, SN 48:8, AN 5:15); the sets of dhammas that came to be known as the 37 *bodhipakkhiya dhamma* (DN 16.3.50/SMPS 19.9, DN 28.3, DN 29.17, MN 103.3, MN 104.5, MN 118.13, MN 149.10/SĀ 305/D 4094, MN 151.14, SN 22:81, SN 22:101, SN 43.5–11, SN 45:155, AN 7:71, AN 8:19, AN 8:28, AN 10:90); noble eightfold path (DN 16.5.27, MN 33.11, AN 4:33, AN 4:34, AN 4:35, AN 5:32, AN 5:196, AN 10:28); path (DN 3.2.21, DN 5.29, DN 16.6.5, MN 56.18, MN 91.36, MN 104.5, SN 8:7, AN 3:125, AN 4:25, AN 4:76, AN 8:13, AN 8:21); seven factors of awakening (DN 28.2, AN 1:74, AN 6:57, AN 10:28, AN 10:61, AN 10:95); five faculties (MN 70.13, AN 6:55, AN 7:56, AN 10:28); four establishments of mindfulness (DN 28.2, MN 12.62, MN 33.12, MN 44.12, SN 22:80, SN 48:8, SN 48:11; AN 5:15, AN 5:136, AN 6:57, AN 10:28, AN 10:61, AN 10:95); four right efforts (MN 44.12, SN 4:4, SN 48.8, SN 48.11, AN 5:15); four bases of psychic potency (DN 16.3.3, SN 4:20, AN 8:70); five hindrances (DN 3.2.21, DN 14.1.13, DN 16.1.17, DN 28.2, MN 56.18, MN 91.36, MN 151.10, SN 8:3, SN 46:54, SN 47:12, AN 4:65, AN 6:45, AN 6:57, AN 8:12, AN 10:61, AN 10:95); three kinds of good conduct (AN10:61); four factors of stream entry (SN 48:8, AN 5:15); five aggregates (MN 9.15, MN 151.11, SN 4:16, SN 35:245, SN 56:11,

[17] Since they are just named and most of them are specific to Buddhism, the assumption must be that the listener already knows them and that they are explained elsewhere. All explanations are indeed found in the EBTs.

AN 3:61, AN 4:254, AN 5:30, AN 6:63, AN 10:27); dependent origination (MN 26.19, MN 98.13, SN 22:57); five lower fetters (SN 47:29, SN 47:30, AN 7:53, AN 8:21); *pātimokkha* (e.g. DN 2, MN 6.2/MĀ 105/EĀ 37.5, MN 53.7, MN 108.14/MĀ 145, SN 47:56, AN 4:12, AN 8:20, SMPS 41.2).[18]

4. **Named specific teachings:**[19] craving being a dart (MN 105.18); whatever is felt is included in suffering (SN 36:11); sexual intercourse destroys the bridge (AN 4:159); affliction being suffering (AN 9:34); the *samādhi* that has knowledge as its fruit (AN 9:37); five sense objects are a confinement (AN 9:42).

5. **Named similes:** the simile of the saw is given at MN 21/MĀ 193 and named at MN 28.9/MĀ 30; the similes of the skeleton, the piece of meat, the grass torch, the pit of coals, the dream, the borrowed goods, the fruits on a tree are given at MN 54.15–21/MĀ 203 and named at MN 22.3/MĀ 200 and AN 5:76; the simile of the butcher's knife and block is given at MN 23.4 and named at MN 22.3 and AN 5:76; the simile of the sword stake is given at SN 5:1 and named at MN 22.3 and AN 5:76.

6. **Verses referred to:** Ud 7:5, cited at SN 41:5.

References

[1] ANĀLAYO. *A Comparative Study of the Majjhima-nikāya*. Dharma Drum Academic Publisher, 2011.

4.3.3 Vivid & realistic

The EBTs convey a picture of India and Indian society at the time that is vivid and realistic; it could not easily have been made up at a later time or in a different society.

The EBTs are full of vivid details of Indian society of the day, such as:

[18] This list of named doctrinal categories could have been expanded greatly. But the present list is probably enough to give a sense of the degree to which the EBTs form an interlocking whole.

[19] For some of these we have not been able to trace the original statement.

1. **Everyday activities:** Arrow making (MN 101.28/MĀ 19), boat building (AN 4:196), chariot riding (MN 21.7/MĀ 193), conveying of greetings (MN 90.3–4/MĀ 212/P 1030), craftsmanship (MN 77.31), dying (MN 7.2/MĀ 93/T 51), debt and interest payment (AN 6:45), dice playing (DN 23.27), fishing (DN 1.3.72), garland making (MN 56.30), herding cows (MN 19.7, MN 19.12, MN 33.15, MN 34.4), making jewelry (AN 3:102), making raft and crossing water (MN 22.13), making sesame oil (MN 126.15), milking cows (MN 126.16), preparing bath powder (MN 39.15), producing fire (DN 23.21, MN 36.17–19, MN 93.11), refining gold (MN 140.20, AN 3:101), spitting (MN 152.7/SĀ 282), swimming (MN 64.8/MĀ 205), taming elephants (MN 125.12/MĀ 198, MN 125.23/MĀ 198), taming horses (MN 65.33/MĀ 194), treating a wound (MN 105.24), warfare (AN 5:75, AN 5:139), wheel making (MN 5.31/MĀ 87/T 49/EĀ 25.6, AN 3:15).

2. **Scenes from everyday life:** Acrobat (SN 47:19), caravan of merchants (DN 23.23), chariot (MN 27.2), chicks hatching (MN 16.27), clothes and accessories (MN 54.3), daughter-in-law (MN 28.10), domestic scene (MN 87.5), elephants playing (MN 35.5), giving travel directions (MN 107.14), leper (MN 75.13), monkey catching (SN 47:7), oil lamp burning (MN 140.24), polite gesture (MN 88.7/MĀ 214), poor man (MN 66.11), protocol when king meets Buddha (MN 89.8/MĀ 213/EĀ 38.10), relay chariots (MN 24.14), rescuing infant (MN 58.7), rich man (MN 66.12), royal elephant (MN 66.7), snake catching (MN 22.10–11), torture (MN 129.4), trumpeter (MN 99.24), weight loss program (SN 3:13).

3. **Environment:** Animals (MN 50.13/MĀ 131/T 66/T 67, MN 66.8/MĀ 192, AN 4:33), autumn sun (MN 46.22), creeper destroying a tree (MN 45.4/MĀ 174), fortress (AN 7:67), lotuses (MN 26.21, MN 152.6), mountain lake (MN 39.21), park (MN 89.4), plantain tree (MN 35.22), sal tree grove (MN 21.8/MĀ 193), towns (SN 55:21), weather (AN 3:35).[20]

[20] See S. Dhammika's forthcoming *Flora & Fauna in Early Buddhist Literature* for a sense of the quantity and detail of such material in the EBTs [1].

These descriptions are often given in detail and appear to be accurate. Even small details, such as the *mañjeṭṭhika* (Vin II 256,26), a disease of sugar cane, has been positively identified as the disease 'red rot', still common in the region today [2, 254]. It would have been hard, perhaps impossible, to reconstruct such details a long time after the event and especially in a different society. Such reconstruction would in all likelihood have included errors or incongruities which would be easily detectable. Moreover, this realistic description is totally different from the past as imagined in other Buddhist literature, which is full of miracles and magic and lacks grounding in everyday realism.

References

[1] DHAMMIKA, S. *Flora & Fauna in Early Buddhist Literature.* Forthcoming.

[2] NEEDHAM, Joseph et al. *Science and Civilisation in China.* Vol. 6. Cambridge University Press, 1954.

4.3.4 Innovation

The EBTs are highly innovative, whereas other Buddhist texts are not.

The EBTs contain a number of ideas that were revolutionary for their time. Most significant among these was the teaching of non-self (*anattā*) [1, 67–70]. Other important innovations included the causal chain of dependent origination [1, 131–137] and the Buddhist version of the law of karma [1, 28, 43, 58–59]. Further, the EBTs contain a large number of new doctrinal structures, such as the four noble truths and the eightfold path, as well as new analyses of the contents of experience, such as the scheme of the five aggregates. Finally, the EBT *pātimokkhas* appear to be a novelty in the history of Indian law [2, 13]. Altogether the EBTs are vastly different from other contemporary literature, especially the Vedas.

Non-EBTs contain very little innovation and are mostly concerned with filling in any perceived gaps in the EBTs, working out their consequences, and systematising them. The EBTs stand out as the only truly innovative layer of Buddhist texts. A natural explanation for this is that the EBTs were the result of the insights of one exceptional person [1, 17].

References

[1] GOMBRICH, Richard. *What the Buddha Thought*. Oxford Centre for Buddhist Studies monographs. Equinox, 2009.

[2] HINÜBER, Oskar VON. "Buddhist Law According to the Theravada-Vinaya: A Survey of Theory and Practice". In: *Journal of the International Association of Buddhist Studies* 18.1 (1995), pp. 7–45.

4.3.5 Claims of incoherence

Scholarship has not succeeded in finding consequential contradictions within the EBTs.

An important challenge to our contention that the EBTs are coherent comes from those who have argued that Buddhism contains fundamental teachings that are hard to reconcile. Probably the most important of these arguments is the claim that Buddhism, specifically the Buddhism of the Pali sources, gives contradictory accounts of the goal of the Buddhist practice, including contradictory accounts of the path of meditation that leads to these goals [1].

This is not the place to assess these claims in detail, but a few general remarks seem called for. A major problem with these claims, here exemplified by those of Griffiths [1], is that they often do not distinguish between EBT and non-EBT material. Griffiths says, "The canonical and commentarial literature will be treated here as a unity ... because the thrust of this paper is structural and philosophical rather than historical, and for such purposes differentiation between canon and commentary is of small importance." This is assuming a point that needs to be proved. In the absence of such proof, it is not possible to ascertain the coherence of the EBTs, or the lack thereof, by relying on non-EBTs. The EBTs need to be considered on their own merits.

Another problem with Griffith's proposition is his reliance on a very limited number of texts from the EBTs. His main reference is to the Satipaṭṭhāna Sutta. However, in establishing any point about the EBTs one needs to consider the literature as a whole.[21] It is our contention that the problems identified by Griffiths and others fall away once this is done.[22]

References

[1] GRIFFITHS, Paul J. "Concentration or insight: the problematic of Theravāda Buddhist Meditation theory". In: *Buddhism: Critical Concepts in Religious Studies*. Vol. II. Routledge, 2005, pp. 154–170.

[2] SUJATO, Bhikkhu. *A History of Mindfulness*. Santipada, 2005. URL: http://santifm.org/santipada/2010/a-history-of-mindfulness/.

[3] SUJATO, Bhikkhu. *A Swift Pair of Messengers*. Santipada, 2000, 2010. URL: http://santipada.org/aswiftpairofmessengers/wp-content/uploads/2010/07/A_Swift_Pair_of_Messengers.pdf.

4.4 Contradictions and oddities not normalised

In many cases there is blatant disagreement between statements found in the EBTs and those found in other Buddhist literature. Despite the glaring inconsistencies, the EBTs were not changed to ensure greater harmony.

4.4.1 Odd details & incongruities

While on the whole the EBTs are highly consistent, they still leave room for many quirky details that convey a realistic flavour; despite the awkwardness they were not removed.

[21] But even his reading of the Satipaṭṭhāna Sutta is not satisfactory, in our opinion. Moreover, the Satipaṭṭhāna Sutta is one of the latest compilations in the Nikāyas [2].

[22] Griffith's main argument is that calm (*samatha*) and insight (*vipassanā*) are two quite distinct types of meditation with distinct goals. However, a full and fair reading of the EBTs shows that calm and insight work together in a complementary fashion; see Sujato's *A Swift Pair of Messengers* for a sustained argument that this is so [3]. Once the path is regarded as unified, it is also natural for the goal of the path to be seen in the same way. The apparent discrepancies in the nature of the goal, as identified by Griffiths, are simply the result of slight differences in the relationship between calm and insight. By failing to distinguish between the EBTs and the ideas of later literature, Griffith has taken conflicts and contradictions that originated in the commentaries and imposed them on the EBTs.

In a number of places the EBTs depict odd or incongruous behaviour, or behaviour that does not fit with how Buddhism or the Buddha is portrayed in other Buddhist texts. This contradicts any ideas of the EBTs being the product of a conscious, artificial propaganda, and is best seen as simply the ordinary realities of life. According to T.W. Rhys Davids [3, x]: "It is a recognised rule of evidence in the courts of law that, if one entry be found in the books kept by a man in the ordinary course of his trade, which entry speaks against himself, then that entry is especially worthy of credence." In other words, since the EBTs give details that contradict later ideas, they are especially trustworthy. It might be thought that this just makes those particular details credible. However, since the EBTs were edited and transmitted through many generations, and there would have been many opportunities to edit the oddities out, there must have been a general principle of conservatism among editors. This makes the entire corpus trustworthy. Examples of such oddities include:

1. It is Rāma, Uddaka's father, who was spiritually attained, not Uddaka (MN 26.16/MĀ 204).[23]

2. Upaka hears the Dhamma from the Buddha but then walks off in the wrong direction (MN 26.25).

3. The Buddha lays down rules and then modifies or even rescinds them (e.g. respectively at Vin IV 72–74 and Vin I 79/83)[24] [2].

4. The Buddha, in the middle of winter, sleeps on a pile of leaves on a cattle track (AN 3:35).

5. The Buddha washes his own feet (MN 31.5).

6. The Buddha personally helps to tend an ill monk (Vin I 304).

---

[23] Of this curious little detail, Wynne says: "The idea must have been in the Buddhist tradition from the beginning, and can only be explained as an attempt to remember an historical fact. There is no other sensible explanation." [4, 65]

[24] In the former case, bhikkhu *pācittiya* 32 was modified a total of seven times. In the latter case, the Buddha first rules that any monk may only be attended on by one novice and then that a wise monk may be attended on by more than one novice.

7. The Buddha is not recognised as such, but is simply seen as a monk (MN 140.3–5/MĀ 162/T 511).

8. The Buddha is disparagingly called various names such as shaveling, recluse-like, menial, dark (DN 3.1.10) and outcast (SN 7:9).

9. A brahman verbally abuses the Buddha (SN 7.2).

10. The Buddha is reluctant to meet with a group of brahman householders who have come to offer him food because they are too noisy (AN 5:30).

11. The Buddha dismisses a group of monks and says he does not want to live near them because they are too noisy, and a group of lay people then causes the Buddha to change his mind (MN 67.2–10/EĀ 45.2/T 137).

12. The Buddha says he is at ease in responding to the calls of nature when he is by himself (AN 8:86).

13. The monk Meghiya not doing his duties towards the Buddha, despite being specifically asked by the Buddha (AN 9:3/MĀ 56).

14. The monks not delighting in a discourse given by the Buddha (MN 1/EĀ 44.6).[25]

15. Ānanda sometimes uses sneaky means to get the Buddha to give a talk (MN 26.3).

16. The monk Bhaddāli refuses to the Buddha's face to keep the *pātimokkha* rule about not eating after midday (MN 65.2–4/MĀ 194/EĀ 49.7).

17. The out of context and seemingly unnecessary episode where king Pasenadi conveys a message to the Buddha from two otherwise unknown sisters (MN 90.3–4/MĀ 212/P 1030).[26]

---

[25] This seems to be the only discourse in which this happens.

[26] It is hard to see how this sort of tangential detail could be the product of artificial construction.

18. The Buddha teaches king Pasenadi how to lose weight (SN 3:13).[27]

19. The Gandhabba Pañcasikha sings a love song to the Buddha, in which he compares his love for a particular female *gandhabba* to the love of arahants for the Dhamma, etc. (DN 21.1.5).

20. The Buddha needs to reflect at length in a vain attempt to help Devadatta (AN 6:62).

21. When Sāriputta dies, his bowl and robe are taken to the Buddha, but there is no mention of relics (SN 47:13).

22. There is no mention in the EBTs of the circumstances of Moggallāna's death.

23. The Buddha says the Sangha seems empty after Sāriputta and Moggallāna have passed away (SN 47:14).

24. King Ajātasattu not knowing where the Buddha is seated in the assembly (DN 2.11).

25. The Buddha complains of having a bad back, and then lies down in the middle of a Dhamma talk (MN 53.5).

26. The Buddha gets tired due to being asked excessively about the rebirth of various people (DN 16.2.8/SMPS 19.17).

27. The Buddha in his old age warms his back in the sun, his limbs are flaccid and wrinkled, and his body stooped (SN 48:41).

28. The Buddha says the rules he has laid down should be kept as they are (DN 16.1.6/SMPS 2.8), but later on he says the minor rules can be abolished (DN 16.6.3/SMPS 41.2).

29. Although the Buddha says the Sangha can abolish the lesser rules after his death (DN 16.6.3/SMPS 41.2), the Sangha does not know which rules he was referring to and therefore decides to keep them all (Vin II 287–288).

[27] This, too, has the marks of natural interaction, rather than conscious construction.

30. The Buddha dies of bloody diarrhoea (DN 16.4.20).[28]

31. Despite spending so much time with the Buddha, Ānanda did not reach arahantship until after the Buddha passed away (Vin II 286).

32. The Pali canonical Vinaya says that only the Dhamma and the Vinaya were recited at the First Council, (Vin II 286–287) but the Dīgha Nikāya commentary blatantly contradicts this by saying that the Abhidhamma was recited too (DN-a I 15).

33. Purāṇa says he will not remember the Dhamma as recited at the First Council, but according to what he himself has heard; this is recorded despite its implications for the diminished authority of the Council (Vin II 289–290).

These episodes, and others, could easily have been edited out, but they were kept despite their awkwardness and their not fitting with later ideas. This indicates that the attitude towards preserving the EBTs was very conservative.

References

[1] ANĀLAYO. "Dabba's Self-cremation in the Saṁyukta-āgama". In: *Buddhist Studies Review* 29.2 (2012), pp. 153–174.

[2] GOMBRICH, Richard. "Popperian Vinaya: Conjecture and refutation in practice". In: *Pramāṇakīrtiḥ, Papers dedicated to Ernst Steinkellner on the Occasion of His 70th Birthday*. Universität Wien, 2007, pp. 203–211.

[3] RHYS DAVIDS, T.W., trans. *Dialogues of the Buddha*. Vol. I. Dialogues of the Buddha: Translated from the Pali of the Dīgha Nikāya. Motilal Banarsidass, 2000.

[4] WYNNE, Alexander. "The Historical Authenticity of Early Buddhist Literature". In: *Vienna Journal of South Asian Studies* XLIX (2005), pp. 35–70. URL: http://www.ocbs.org/images/stories/awynne2005wzks.pdf.

---

[28] This episode, however realistic it appears, seems to be absent from most of the other versions of this sutta [1, 165 note 68].

4.4.2 Later texts are obvious

Later texts or passages typically reveal themselves in multiple different ways, which indicates that the ancient Buddhists were not interested in composing realistic fakes.

In identifying later additions to the canon, it is usually possible to use multiple independent criteria. For example, in the case of MN 111, the Anupada Sutta, the following 5 criteria are relevant [2]:

1. No known parallels in non-Pali EBTS;
2. Extravagant praise of Sāriputta, not found elsewhere in the EBTS and akin to the flowery and exaggerated language of other Buddhist texts;[29]
3. Textual duplication and redundancy, such as *upekkhā* being mentioned twice as a *jhāna* factor for both the third and the fourth *jhāna*;
4. Abhidhamma type vocabulary, not found elsewhere in the EBTS, such as *anupadavavaṭṭhita*;
5. Juxtaposition of different literary styles, specifically one Sutta style list of *jhāna* factors connected with *ca* and one Abhidhamma style list of factors without *ca*.

Moreover, the redactors could easily have hidden their additions by careful editing, but they didn't. Where they added new material, they did so without attempting to disguise it, and sometimes the additions are acknowledged as such in the commentaries, e.g., the final verses of the Mahāparinibbāna Sutta (DN-a II 615) [3, 224], all the verses of the Lakkhaṇa Sutta (DN-a III 922), and the entire Bakkula Sutta (MN-a IV 197).

Similarly, there are many Suttas that are set in the time following the Buddha's demise, and this is acknowledged in the texts.[30]

[29] For an example of flowery language see section 4.2.4 above

[30] E.g. MN 94.32, MN 84.10, MN 108.1/MĀ 145. The latest text added to the EBTS is possibly the dialogue with King Muṇḍa in AN 5:50/EĀ 32.7, which may have taken place a few decades after the Buddha's death. There are also Suttas spoken by disciples that give no

Both the EBTs and the later tradition, then, quite readily acknowledge that some discourses were not spoken by the Buddha. In some cases, such as the final verses of the Mahāparinibbāna Sutta, this could not have been otherwise, as the context is after the Buddha's passing away. In other cases, however, such as the verses of the Lakkhaṇa Sutta, even though the Sutta features the Buddha himself, the commentary is still happy to acknowledge that the verse were added later. The fact, therefore, that in the majority of cases there is no acknowledgement of lateness tends to authenticate these text as having the historical Buddha as their origin.

References

[1] ANĀLAYO. *A Comparative Study of the Majjhima-nikāya.* Dharma Drum Academic Publisher, 2011.

[2] ANĀLAYO. *The Dawn of Abhidharma.* Forthcoming.

[3] ANĀLAYO. "The Historical Value of the Pāli Discourses". In: *Indo-Iranian Journal* 55 (2012), pp. 223–253.

[4] HINÜBER, Oskar VON. "Hoary past and hazy memory. On the history of early Buddhist texts". In: *Journal of the International Association of Buddhist Studies* 29.2 (2006), pp. 193–210.

4.4.3 Life of the Buddha

The EBTs are interested in the Dhamma, while after the Buddha's death interest shifted to his life story.

The EBTs display little interest in the Buddha's biography. This is in stark contrast to other Buddhist literature [3, 214–215]. This is most naturally

indication of whether the Buddha is alive or dead (e.g. MN 52; although both Chinese parallels to this Sutta, MĀ 217 and T 92, do state that the Buddha had passed away). The opening section of such Suttas is similar to those where the Buddha is specifically said to have attained *parinibbāna*, in the sense that the whereabouts of the Buddha is not mentioned. (Other Suttas spoken by disciples mention the whereabouts of the Buddha in the narrative introduction, e.g. MN 5/MĀ 87/T 49/EĀ 25.6 and MN 9/MĀ 29/SĀ 344.) [1, 310] This, combined with other indications, suggests that these Suttas were spoken after the Buddha's death. In the case of MN 52 one such other indication is that the protagonist came from the town of Pāṭaliputta, which was just a village called Pāṭaligāma in the Buddha's lifetime, see section 1.1.5 above and [4, 202–206].

explained if the EBTs stem mainly from the historical Buddha himself. He was interested in teaching the Dhamma, not telling his life story. And where the Buddha does speak of his own life, it is always to give a teaching on how he practised to reach awakening, presumably to set an example to be emulated.[31] Those around him knew him personally and did not need a lengthy biography. Only after he died was there a need to develop a biographical literature, beginning with the Mahāparinibbāna Sutta, then the Khandhakas, then the full-fledged biographies, such as the Mahāvastu, the Lalitavistara, and the Jātaka Nidāna.

Moreover, the few details that the EBTs give of the Buddha's life frequently contradict the later legends:

1. His practices in past lives "did not lead to Awakening" (DN 19.61, MN 83.21/MĀ 67/EĀ 50.4/P 1030), vs. practising as a *bodhisatta* for an incalculable period (JN 25–61).

2. In past lives he had no notion of being a *bodhisatta* (MN 81/MĀ 63/P 1030, MN 83/MĀ 67/EĀ 50.4/P 1030, AN 3:15), vs. taking the *bodhisatta* vow under the mythological Buddha Dīpaṅkara an incalculable long time ago (JN 17–18).

3. He left home motivated by seeing the danger in human violence and social disturbance (Snp 4:15, verses 936–938) and to seek freedom from suffering and death (MN 26.12/MĀ 204), vs. becoming a *bodhisatta* out of compassion (JN 17–18).

4. He left home while his parents were crying (MN 26.14/MĀ 204), vs. leaving in the middle of the night while his family was asleep (JN 82–84).

5. Siddhattha is a *bodhisatta* only after leaving home to become an ascetic,[32] vs. being a *bodhisatta* for an incalculable period of time (JN 25–61) [2].

[31] See MN 4/EĀ 31.1, MN 12/T 757, MN 19/MĀ 102, MN 26/MĀ 204, MN 36, MN 85, MN 128/MĀ 72.

[32] Except in MN 123, the Acchariyabbhuta Sutta. However, there is great variation in the number of factors included in the existing versions of this Sutta, indicating that it was added to at a late date.

6. Struggled in meditation (MN 128/MĀ 72, MN 19/MĀ 102, MN 4/EĀ 31.1), vs. smooth progress (JN 90).

7. Practised austerities due to wrong view (MN 85.10), vs. practised them to show the world his perseverance and endeavour (JN 89).

8. No mention of compassion as motivation until after Awakening (compare pre-Awakening MN 26.13/MĀ 204 with post-Awakening MN 26.21), vs. compassion being the motivation for becoming a *bodhisatta* (JN 17–18) [1, 179–181].

9. The Buddha walked from Bodhgaya to Benares to start teaching (MN 26.25), vs. going to Benares in half a day, implying the use of psychic powers (JN 109).

10. Sakya being a small republic subject to Kosala (MN 89.19/MĀ 213/EĀ 38.10/T 1451/P 1035),[33] vs. Sakya being a kingdom with the *bodhisatta*'s father as king and Kapilavatthu as the enormous and magnificent capital (JN 69, 76–77).

11. The Buddha attained awakening (*sammāsambodhi*, SN 56:11), vs. the Buddha attained omniscience (*sabbaññutā*) (JN 99).

Again, such details could easily have been removed from the EBTs. That they were kept despite the contradictions with other Buddhist texts, again shows the conservatism of the Sangha in keeping the EBTs as unchanged as possible.

References

[1] ANĀLAYO. *A Comparative Study of the Majjhima-nikāya*. Dharma Drum Academic Publisher, 2011.

[2] ANĀLAYO. *The Genesis of the Bodhisattva Ideal*. Hamburg Buddhist Studies. Hamburg University Press, 2010.

[3] BAREAU, André. "Archaeological Research on Ancient Buddhist Sites". In: *When Did the Buddha Live?: The Controversy on the Dating of the Historical Buddha*. Bibliotheca Indo-Buddhica. Sri Satguru Publications, 1995.

[33] The Buddha calls himself a Kosalan, implying that the Sakyans are Kosalan subjects.

4.5 Supernormal elements

> *The supernormal aspects of the EBTs can be explained as due partly to the world-view integral to EBT doctrine and partly to editorial decisions made to enhance the relative prestige of Buddhism.*

From the perspective of a modern reader, the EBTs may seem to contain a number of supernatural elements that diminish the historical value of the whole genre. Steven Collins comments:

> "In the texts of the Pali Canon the Buddha is very frequently depicted as interacting with gods and other supernaturals, often giving them doctrinal talks. Many modern historians, who of course must be professionally at the very least agnostic about the existence of supernaturals, assume that one can ignore the nature of the Buddha's interlocutors but still accept what he is depicted as saying as evidence of 'his ideas'. But if later generations could invent gods for the Buddha to talk to they could also invent what he said to them. We have no way of distinguishing between transmission and invention." [1]

The assertion on which Collins' argument rests, that the Buddha is depicted in the Pali Canon as "very frequently giving them (the 'supernaturals') doctrinal talks," is simply not true. Of all the 186 Suttas of the Dīgha and Majjhima Nikāyas, there is only a single one of which this is true, the Sakkapañha Sutta (DN 21).[34]

The truth is almost the exact reverse of what Collins would have us believe. Apart from the significant evidence from the Dīgha and Majjhima Nikāyas, an analysis of one of the main sections of the Canon that deals with supernormal beings, the Sagāthā Vagga of the Saṁyutta Nikāya, shows that they are almost exclusively confined to circumstantial material found in the narrative sections. The Sagāthā Vagga contains over 200 Suttas in which the Buddha is seen in conversation with divine beings. However, in only

---

[34] It is also partly true of MN 49, which in the main is a story of a meeting between the Buddha and Brahmā. This Sutta does contain some doctrinal material, but it is far from being a typical teaching Sutta. Then there are MN 37 and MN 50, both of which are story type Suttas, presenting Mahāmoggallāna, one of the Buddha's chief disciples, in conversation with gods. In both cases, especially in MN 50, the narrative element far outweighs the sparse doctrinal content.

21 of these does the actual conversation, as opposed to the surrounding material, suggest that one of the parties is non-human.[35] Further, 15 of these 21 are conversations with Māra. But since Māra in the EBTs is often a name for a psychological state,[36] it is likely that this is so in the majority (perhaps all) of these cases too. This leaves us with only six Suttas out of more than 200. But even this number does not give a fair representation of the state of affairs. All of these six Suttas consist of no more than the exchange of a few inspirational verses. They either lack doctrinal content completely or it is very limited. That is, we are probably not dealing with the sort of core doctrinal material that might be considered untouchable.

The notion that discussions between the Buddha and supernormal beings are rare or absent is also implied by a passage in the Mahāparinibbāna Sutta (DN 16.2.17). The Buddha is approached by the brightly dressed and flamboyant Licchavi princes, and, apparently amused, he says to the monks that for those who have never seen the gods of the Tāvatiṁsa realm, now is their chance, since they look just like these Licchavis! If the gods were visiting the Buddha regularly, filling the entire monastery with radiance, as the stock passage describes it, the monks could hardly have avoided noticing this.

This quick survey does not cover all the Suttas in the Pali Canon in which the Buddha is seen conversing with supernormal beings, but it probably comprises the vast majority of them. What we find, then, is that supernormal beings are no more than peripheral and mostly mentioned either in stories or in the narrative material that surrounds the core doctrinal content. In other words, whatever enhancement the EBTs underwent at the hands of redactors was limited to the circumstantial material and did not affect the core message of the Buddha's teaching.[37]

---

[35] In 140 Suttas only the narrative framework makes it clear that supernormal beings are involved. In a further 47 Suttas nothing at all is said about supernormal beings, but their presence is implied by the fact that these Suttas are included in this collection.

[36] See for instance Snp 3:2, where Māra's armies are metaphors for psychological states. Similarly, "Māra's daughters" at SN 4.25 are named Taṇhā, Rāgā, and Rati (Craving, Lust, and Desire), and are therefore also metaphorical.

[37] And it seems to us that this situation probably holds true for many, perhaps most, of the supernormal phenomena described in the EBTs.

We do not mean to deny that the EBTs express a world-view in which supernormal phenomena are a part. Indeed, it is likely that this very world-view was partly responsible for the inclusion of such material in the narrative sections. That, and the prestige that this may have given the Suttas in the eyes of the intended audience, is sufficient to explain why it is there. There is no good reason for thinking that the existence of these elements shows that the transmission of the core doctrinal content has been unreliable.

Regardless of the actual status of supernormal beings, powers, or events in the life of the Buddha, the argument by Collins is of a peculiar sort. He moves from saying that later generations "could have" invented the Buddha's statements—a straw man argument, since no-one disputes something so obviously true—to the general assertion that we have "no way" to distinguish transmission from invention. As we have shown throughout this essay, there are in fact many ways of distinguishing invention from transmission. Moreover, these are little different from the kinds of ordinary distinctions that we make in all forms of discourse. For example, consider the frequent evocations of "God" by American politicians. Do we assume that, if we are professionally agnostic towards the existence of a creator deity, we have no grounds for knowing whether any statements by that politician are true? Of course not. We take their religious beliefs as religious beliefs, and do not expect to find hard evidence for them. And we evaluate their factual claims by reference to knowable facts, just as we would do for anyone else.

Yet instead of making this sort of basic distinction, Collins sees the mention of supernormal elements as a reason for dismissing the EBTs outright, so that the very possibility of clearer understanding is denied. The proper course of a careful investigator, rather, would be to consider the nature and form of the supernormal elements, and to clarify the roles that they play within the literature.

References

[1] COLLINS, Steven. *'Theravāda civilization(s)'? Periodizing its history*. 2013. URL: http://theravadaciv.org/wp-content/uploads/2013/02/Theravda-civilisations.pdf.

4.6 Structure

4.6.1 The structure of the Saṃyutta

The Saṁyutta is structured in such a way as to appear to be the original canonical collection of central doctrines.

The EBTs emphasise the centrality of teachings such as the four noble truths, dependent origination, and the *bodhipakkhiya dhammas*. The early community recited and memorised such teachings, organising them into the ancestor of today's Saṁyutta/Saṁyuktas. The Saṁyutta as a whole is shaped after the pattern of the broadest of all the teaching frameworks, the four noble truths (MN 28.2/MĀ 30).

The Saṁyutta Nikāya/Āgama collects Suttas (usually) by topic, and those topics neatly represent the four noble truths: the aggregates, senses, and elements under the truth of suffering; dependent origination under the truths of origination and cessation; and the subject of mental development under the truth of the path [2] [3, 48] [4] [5] [6]. If the Saṁyutta Nikāya/Āgama is the earliest collection of Suttas—as suggest by noted scholars such as Yin Shun [3, 23]—from which the other Nikāyas/Āgamas evolved, then the Saṁyutta structure may be a literal implementation of Sāriputta's statement that all good teachings are included in the four noble truths (MN 28.2/MĀ 30).

The Saṁyutta structure also closely relates to the 37 *bodhipakkhiya dhammas*, which make up most of the last section of this work, that dealing with the path. In several places the EBTs present the *bodhipakkhiya dhammas* as being a summary or the essence of the Buddha's teachings (SN 22:81), and the Buddha exhorts the Sangha to keep an accurate memory of them.[38]

That the content of the collection in this way is reflected in its structure is another indication that the Saṁyutta/Saṁyuktas are an integrated whole stemming from a single source.

Finally, it has also been proposed that the first three of the 9 *aṅgas* should be identified with the proto-Saṁyutta, based on a statement by Asanga and on the pattern of distribution of texts within these collections [3, 2.45, 3.42, 4.29]. This would mean that the first three *aṅgas* formed

---

[38] MN 103.4–8, MN 104.5, DN 16.3.50/SMPS 19.7, DN 29.17.

a sub-structure within the proto-Saṁyutta. If this is correct, then we can discern the earliest form of a Buddhist "canon", before the current organisation of texts into Nikāyas/Āgamas.[39]

References

[1] ANĀLAYO. *A Comparative Study of the Majjhima-nikāya*. Dharma Drum Academic Publisher, 2011.

[2] CHOONG, Mun-keat. *The Fundamental Teachings of Early Buddhism: A Comparative Study Based on the Sūtrāṅga Portion of the Pali Saṁyutta-Nikāya and the Chinese Saṁyuktāgama*. Harrassowitz, 2000.

[3] SUJATO, Bhikkhu. *A History of Mindfulness*. Santipada, 2005. URL: `http://santifm.org/santipada/2010/a-history-of-mindfulness/`.

[4] YINSHUN. *Yuanshi Fojiao Shengdian zhi Jicheng [The Formation of Early Buddhist Texts]*. Zhengwen Chubanshe, Taipei, 1971.

[5] YINSHUN. "Za-ahan-jing Bulei zhi Zhengbian [Re-edition of the Grouped Structure of SA]". In: *Za-ahan Jing-Lun Huibian [Combined Edition of Sūtra and Śāstra of Saṁyuktāgama]*. Vol. I. Zhengwen Chubanshe, 1991, pp. 1–74.

[6] YINSHUN. "Za-ahan-jing Han-Ba duizhaobiao [A Comparative Table of SA to the Pali texts]". In: FSA *(Foguang Tripitaka)*. Vol. 4. 1983, pp. 3–72.

4.6.2 Fractal structure

> *The EBTs possess a strongly fractal structure, that is, they are self-similar at different levels. Such structures are characteristic of organic growth, not of artificial construction.*

A fractal is a mathematical set that generates an object or pattern that is self-similar, that is, exactly or approximately similar at all scales. Unlike normal geometric patterns, fractals retain detail no matter how small the scale is [1] [2].

Both the content and the form of the EBTs exhibit fractal characteristics. The best example in terms of content is the four noble truths. These may be expressed at the smallest level of linguistic meaning, the word: *dukkha, samudaya, nirodha, magga*. Each of these terms may be expanded

[39] This idea, however, has been critiqued by Anālayo [1, 697–700].

indefinitely, thus displaying an ever increasing amount of detail (see e.g. MN 28/MĀ 30 and MN 141/MĀ 31/T 32/EĀ 27.1). At its largest scale, the four noble truths form the structure of the Saṁyutta Nikāya and, according to MN 28/MĀ 30, encompass all good teachings, that is, the Dhamma as a whole.

Likewise, the formal linguistic features of the EBTs exhibit fractal features. An example is the use of repetition. These occur at the level of the word, the sentence, the paragraph, the passage, the text, and the group of texts.

The resemblance to fractals is not coincidental. A fractal is formed through the recursive iteration of a simple operation. This is analogous to the manner in which complex Dhamma analyses are produced through repeated questioning of the previous statement ("And what, monks, is...?"; again see MN 28/MĀ 30). Moreover, a crucial benefit of such fractal patterns is that they are compressible. It is possible to learn the essence of the Dhamma in a few words, and all expansions exemplify the same pattern.

Such patterns are frequently observed in nature, and are an outstanding feature of organic as opposed to artificial growth. The fractal features of the EBTs, therefore, suggest that they also grew organically and holistically, not through the artificial bolting together of elements from different origins. The most obvious way that this would have happened is through a gradual expansion in details and contexts of the earliest teachings. The initial impetus for teaching may have been a particular insight, but an insight that allowed virtually endless variations and expansions in its exposition. This differs from non-EBT Buddhist literature, where we frequently see early elements juxtaposed with entirely different formulations.

References

[1] THORNBURY, Scott. *F is for Fractal.* 29 April 2012. URL: http://scottthornbury.wordpress.com/2012/04/29/f-is-for-fractal/.

[2] WEISSTEIN, Eric W. "*Fractal.*" *From MathWorld—A Wolfram Web Resource.* 2013. URL: http://mathworld.wolfram.com/Fractal.html.

CHAPTER 5

Archaeology

5.1 Overview

The archaeology of the first few centuries BCE strongly and consistently reveals the widespread presence of Buddhism in India.

Towns, cities, and other sites described in the EBTs have for the most part been identified through archaeological excavations. Some of the findings go back to the time of Asoka or even before. Significantly, most of the sites were discovered and understood with the aid of the texts [1, 21–26, 32–33, 205–213], but the sites themselves have generally provided independent evidence of their identity.[1] The paucity of archaeological evidence for the period before Asoka is due to the fact that buildings were constructed of mud and timber [3, 142 and note 3] [4, 165] [5, 66, 68, 204, 206–207], and because the Mauryan period, starting in about 300 BCE, marks the beginning of the script and picture age in Indian Archaeology [3, 141].

According to Härtel, places of importance for Buddhist history have been "rebuilt again and again on the same ground" and "no archaeologist will dare to remove the mostly solid remains of the upper level". He concludes that "the hope to recover the original structures and ruins of a town or habitation of the time of the Buddha, let us say Kapilavastu, is almost zero" [3, 142]. This, then, would seem to be the reason for the very limited pre-Mauryan archaeological finds.

1 E.g. Lumbinī (Asokan pillar), Sāvatthī [2, 409], Vesālī [2, 443], Kosambī [2, 394–396], and Nāḷandā [2, 469].

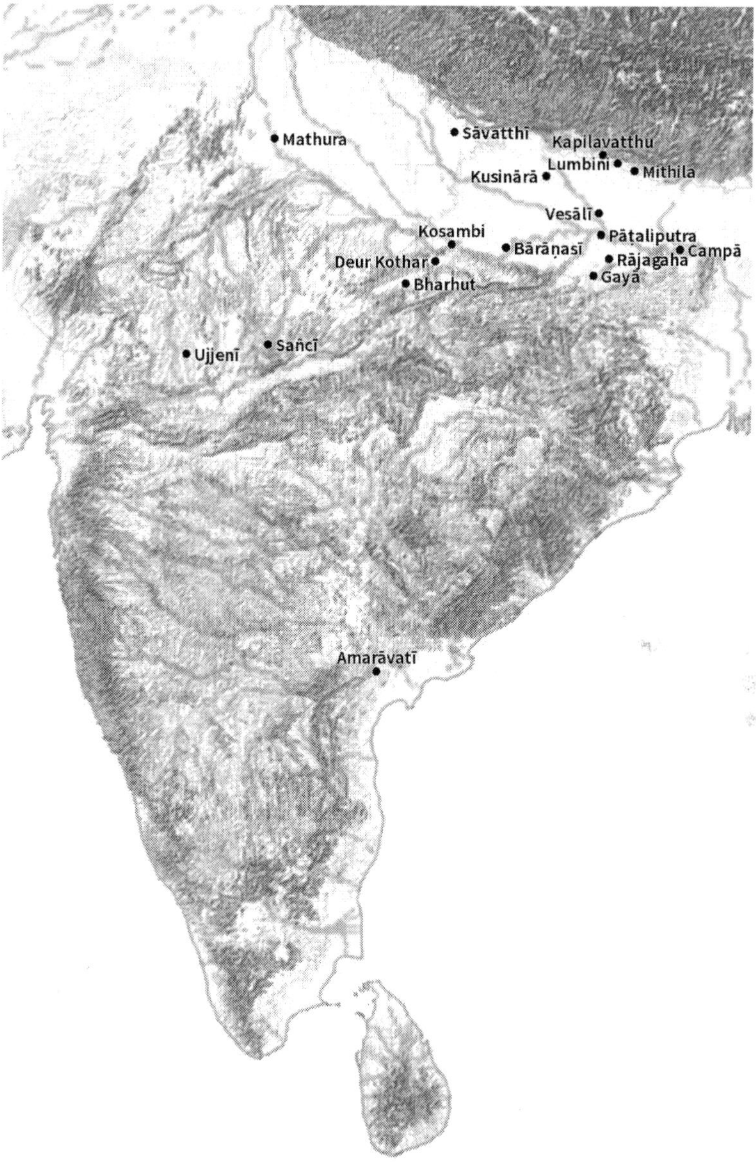

Figure 5.1: Towns and sites associated with the Buddha and the spread of Buddhism.

References

[1] ALLEN, C. *The Buddha and the Sahibs: The Men Who Discovered India's Lost Religion.* John Murray, 2002.

[2] CUNNINGHAM, Alexander. *The ancient geography of India.* Trübner and Co., 1871. URL: http://www.archive.org/stream/cu31924016181111#page/n3/mode/2up.

[3] HÄRTEL, Herbert. "Archaeological Research on Ancient Buddhist Sites". In: *When Did the Buddha Live?: The Controversy on the Dating of the Historical Buddha.* Bibliotheca Indo-Buddhica. Sri Satguru, 1995.

[4] KULKE, Hermann. "Some considerations on the significance of Buddha's date for the history of North India". In: *When Did the Buddha Live?: The Controversy on the Dating of the Historical Buddha.* Bibliotheca Indo-Buddhica. Sri Satguru, 1995.

[5] MCCRINDLE, J.W. and JAIN, R.C. *McCrindle's Ancient India: as described by Megasthenes and Arrian.* Trübner and Co., 1876. URL: http://www.archive.org/stream/ancientindiaasd01mccrgoog#page/n6/mode/2up.

5.2 Asokan edicts

Asoka's edicts reveal the presence of Buddhism as a major religious movement across India less than two centuries after the Buddha.

The Asokan edicts are dated to about 150 years after the Buddha. They are the earliest datable epigraphic evidence in Indian history,[2] and the earliest significant archaeological finds in the middle Ganges area. They record the deeds and proclamations of the Mauryan emperor Asoka, who converted to Buddhism during his reign. Buddhism must therefore have been a major and growing force in Indian religion for a considerable period before Asoka. Elements in the inscriptions that agree with the EBTs, some of which are explicit references, include:

[2] According to Gombrich (personal communication), "there are fragments of brāhmī inscriptions" that could be earlier than the Asokan edicts, but that have not yet been securely dated.

- **RE 1 (Girnār version):**[3] No living beings are to be killed or offered in sacrifice [1] [7, 64].
- **RE 2 (Girnār):** Asoka made provisions "everywhere" (*sarvata vijitamhi*) for the medical treatment of both humans and animals, and he had wells dug and trees planted for their use [1] [7, 66].
- **RE 3 (Girnār):** "Respect for mother and father is good; generosity to friends, acquaintances, relatives, brahmans and ascetics is good; nonviolence to animals is good; moderation in spending and possessions is good." [1] [7, 68]
- **RE 4 (Girnār):** Overlaps in part with RE 3, but adds "proper behaviour towards relatives, brahmans and ascetics, and respect for the aged." Also "to instruct in the Dhamma is the highest work." [1] [7, 70]
- **RE 5 (Kālsī):** "Good deeds (*kayāna* (= *kalyāṇa*)) are difficult to perform" and "bad acts (*pāpa*) are easy to commit", apparently quoting the EBTs (see Ud 5:8) [1] [7, 74].
- **RE 6 (Girnār):** Asoka considers the welfare of the whole world (*sarva-loka-hita*) to be his duty [1] [7, 78].
- **RE 8 (Girnār):** Going on a Dhamma tour (*dhaṁma-yātā*), Asoka visited "*sambodhi*" (Bodhgaya). There was Dhamma instruction (*dhaṁmānusasṭī*) and Dhamma questions (*dhama-paripuchā*) with the country people [1] [7, 84–85].
- **RE 9 (Girnār):** Asoka expresses his disapproval of excessive "auspicious" (*maṁgala*) ceremonies (which is comparable to what is truly auspicious according to the Maṅgala Sutta, Snp 2:4) and instead (along the same lines as RE 3 and RE 4) favours proper behaviour towards slaves and servants, respect to teachers, restraint in regard to animals, generosity towards brahmans and ascetics, all typical

[3] In the following PE stands for Pillar Edict, MPE for Minor Pillar Edict, RE for Rock Edict, and MRE for Minor Rock Edict. The numbering system follows that used by Dhammika [1].

Buddhist virtues. This edict (as well as RE 11) also says that "there is no gift like the gift of the Dhamma", which is likely to be a quote from the EBTs (see AN 9:5 or Dhp 354) [1] [7, 86].

- **RE 11 (Girnār):** Many of the same points as mentioned above in RE 9 [1] [7, 92].
- **RE 12 (Girnār):** "One should listen to and respect the doctrine of others." [1] [7, 94]
- **RE 13 (Kālsī):** Asoka repents his conquering of the Kāliṅgas. He states that "conquest by Dhamma is the best conquest," echoing the conquest of a wheel-turning monarch described at DN 17.1.8–9 [1] [7, 98].
- **Kaliṅga RE 1 (Dhaulī):** Asoka tells his officials that they should practice the middle (*majhaṁ paṭipādayema*). This would seem to be a reference to the Buddhist middle way [2, 130]. Immediately following this he says that "one does not act right when acting from envy, anger, cruelty, hurry, indifference, laziness, or fatigue." [1] [7, 110–111]
- **Kaliṅga RE 2 (Jaugaḍa):** Asoka says his subjects should feel "the king acts towards us as a father would; he feels for us as he feels for himself; we are to the king as his own children." This passage echoes the sentiment in the EBT description of the ideal king at DN 17.1.21/ SMPS 34.25 [1] [7, 118].
- **MRE 1 (Gavīmaṭh):** Asoka calls himself an *upāsaka*, a Buddhist lay disciple [7, 53]; a Śākya, one who belongs to the Buddha's (spiritual) family (Rūpnāth version) [7, 54]; and possibly a Budhaśake, a Sakyan of the Buddha (Maskī version) [7, 54]; and says he has visited the Sangha [1] [7, 53].
- **MRE 2 (Yerrāguḍi):** One should respect mother and father, as well as teachers (*garu*); one should have mercy for animals; one should speak the truth; pupils (*aṁtevāsi*) should respect their teachers (*ācariya*)—all typical Buddhist virtues [1] [7, 57].

- **MRE 3 (Bairāt):** Asoka honors (*abhivādetūnaṁ* (= *abhivādetvā*)) the Sangha and hopes it has little affliction (*apābādhata*) and is dwelling at ease (*phāsu-vihālata*), both expressions being from the EBTs. He expresses his respect (*gālava*) and faith (*prasāda*) in the "*budha dhaṁma saṁgha*", and then says that all that was spoken by the Buddha was well-spoken (*subhāsita*). He speaks of "the long duration of the true dhamma (*sadhaṁma*)", apparently quoting the EBTs (see e.g. SN 16:13). He then lists a number of Buddhist texts (*dhaṁma-paliyāya*) as recommended study curriculum: Vinaya-samukasa, Aliya-vasāni, Anāgata-bhayāni, Muni-gāthā, Moneya-sūta, Upatisa-pasina, Lāghul-ovāda. The last of these is specifically said to concern lying, which is also the subject matter of this Sutta in the EBTs [7, 132–135]. There is some disagreement among scholars as to the exact identity of some of these [4, 235–236] [6, 169–170], since Buddhist texts frequently go by various titles. There is, however, no question of having to seek outside the EBTs to find them [1]. This edict also uses the following EBT terminology: *bhikhu*, *bhikhuni*, *upāsaka*, and *upāsikā*, and the Buddha is called *bhagavat* [7, 135].

- **PE 2:**[4] "Dhamma consists of doing few bad deeds, many good deeds, being compassionate, generous, truthful, and pure." Asoka further says that "many benefits have been conferred by him on bipeds, quadrupeds, birds and fish." [1] [7, 146]

- **PE 3:** "One should regard it thus: These are the ways to bad conduct, that is, fierceness, cruelty, anger, pride, envy. Let me not be ruined by them." [1] [7, 148]

- **PE 4:** Asoka abolishes the death penalty [2, 129] [5, 200–209].

- **PE 5:** Asoka prohibits violence against and the killing of various animals [1] [7, 154, 156].

- **PE 7 (Delhi-Toprā):** Asoka summarises all his good deeds. He mentions the Jains (*nigaṁṭha*) and the Ājīvakas, both found in the EBTs

[4] For the pillar edicts the variations between the different versions are so minor it seems unnecessary to indicate which version we are using [7, 142].

[1] [7, 164]. He says that, "People's progress in Dhamma is achieved in two ways, by Dhamma rules and by conviction. Rules count for little; most is by conviction." [2, 131] [7, 166–167] Otherwise this edict mostly repeats what he has already proclaimed elsewhere [1] [7, 162, 164, 166, 168].

- **MPE 1 (Lumbinī):** "Here the Buddha, Sakya-muni, was born" (A: *hida budhe jāte sakya-munī ti*; B: *hida bhagavaṁ jāte ti*). Asoka then remits the taxation of the inhabitants of Lumbinī [1] [7, 122].

- **MPE 2 (Sārnāth):** Asoka condemns schism in the Sangha. He says that any monk or nun who causes such a schism is to be disrobed [7, 130]. This shows Asoka's remarkable concern for the well-being of the Sangha. A variety of specialist EBT terms are employed: *bhikhu-saṁgha, bhikhuni-saṁgha, sāsana, upāsaka, anuposatha, saṁgha bheta, saṁgha samaga* (Sāñcī version), *cila-thitīka* (Sāñcī) [1] [7, 130–131].

- **PE at Nigālī-sāgar:** Mentions the stupa of Buddha Konāgamana and that Asoka paid his respects there [7, 124].

Gombrich makes the point that Asoka, like the Buddha, used current terminology in new ways, thereby turning worldly pursuits into Dhamma pursuits, all of which have strong Buddhist overtones. Perhaps Asoka was imitating the Buddha [2, 130].

Although much of the content of the Asokan edicts is not specifically Buddhist, the overall tenor is Buddhist. For example, many of the virtues listed above are similar in substance and detail to those of the EBTs [2, 130] [3, Introduction, ch. 5]. Moreover, and significantly, there is nothing in these edicts that contradicts the teachings in the EBTs.

References

[1] DHAMMIKA, S., trans. *The Edicts of King Asoka*. 1994–2013. URL: http://www.accesstoinsight.org/lib/authors/dhammika/wheel386.html.

[2] GOMBRICH, Richard. *Theravāda Buddhism: A Social History from Ancient Benares to Modern Colombo*. The Library of Religious Beliefs and Practices Series. Routledge & Kegan Paul, 2006.

[3] HULTZSCH, E., ed. *Inscriptions of Asoka New Edition by E(ugen) Hultzsch, Oxford 1925. (angl.)* Corpus inscriptionum indicarum. 1. Clarendon Press, 1925.

[4] LAMOTTE, Étienne. *History of Indian Buddhism: From the Origins to the Śaka Era.* Publications de l'Institut orientaliste de Louvain. Université catholique de Louvain, Institut orientaliste, 1988.

[5] NORMAN, K.R. *Collected Papers I.* The Pali Text Society, 1990.

[6] RHYS DAVIDS, T.W. *Buddhist India.* Putnam, 1903. URL: `http://fsnow.com/text/buddhist-india/`.

[7] SEN, A., trans. *Aśoka's edicts.* Institute of Indology series. Indian Publicity Society for the Institute of Indology, 1956. URL: `http://asi.nic.in/asi_books/5282.pdf`.

5.3 Barabar caves

The inscriptions on these caves confirm the existence of a religious order frequently mentioned in the EBTs.

Asoka and his grandson Dasaratha made rock-cut caves for the ascetics of the Ājīvaka sect in the 3rd century BCE [1, 317]. The Ājīvakas feature frequently in the EBTs.[5]

References

[1] LAMOTTE, Étienne. *History of Indian Buddhism: From the Origins to the Śaka Era.* Publications de l'Institut orientaliste de Louvain. Université catholique de Louvain, Institut orientaliste, 1988.

5.4 Bodh Gaya

The place of the Buddha's Awakening is a rich archaeological site that dates back at least to Asoka.

According to Härtel, the *vajrāsana* ("the diamond seat"), meant to mark the spot where the Buddha attained awakening, is likely to be the oldest archaeological relic at Bodhgaya and is dated to the time of Asoka [1, 144].

[5] Eg. AN 3:72, AN 5:293, AN 6:57, MN 5.

The artwork on the railings at Bodhgaya seem to be from the 2nd century BCE. It is more rudimentary than that in other locations [2, 411]. The scenes depicted are given in less detail, and thus they are often hard to identify [2, 411]. Nevertheless, some of the artwork can clearly be identified as Buddhist. For instance the lotus, an important early Buddhist symbol that often refers to the Buddha's birth, features frequently [2, 408]. Other Buddhist motifs are as follows:

1. **From the EBTs:** first meditation (MN 36.31) [2, 405]; first teaching, symbolised by the *dhammacakka* (SN 56:11/SĀ 379/T 109/T 110/EĀ 19.2/P 747/P 1003) [2, 405]; Indra's visit (DN 21/DĀ 14/T 15/MĀ 134) [2, 405]; *parinibbāna,* symbolised by stupa (DN 16.6.7–9/DĀ 2/T 5/T 6/T 7/T 1451/SMPS 42.11–18) [2, 405].

2. **From non-EBTs:** grass cutter's gift (JN 93) [2, 405]; wonder of parting the water and walking on dry ground (Vin I 32) [2, 405]; return to Kapilavatthu (Vin I 82–83 and JN 118–119) [2, 405]; gift of Jetavana (Vin II 158–159) [2, 405]; homage to Buddha by Pārileyyaka elephant (Vin I 353) [2, 405]; a dozen Jātakas (7 unidentified) [2, 405].

References

[1] HÄRTEL, Herbert. "Archaeological Research on Ancient Buddhist Sites". In: *When Did the Buddha Live?: The Controversy on the Dating of the Historical Buddha.* Bibliotheca Indo-Buddhica. Sri Satguru, 1995.

[2] LAMOTTE, Étienne. *History of Indian Buddhism: From the Origins to the Śaka Era.* Publications de l'Institut orientaliste de Louvain. Université catholique de Louvain, Institut orientaliste, 1988.

5.5 Deur Kothar

Deur Kothar (or Deorkothar), a little known Buddhist site, is one of the oldest sources of material evidence for Buddhism.

This Buddhist monument contains some of the earliest stupas, and it includes Asokan-era writing, rock shelters, simple art, an Asokan pillar, and Northern Black Polished Ware. It probably stems from the beginnings of

Buddhist popular monuments (Mishra suggests the 3rd century BCE [2]), which were greatly advanced by the time of Bhārhut, about a century later. The use of mainly abstract motifs is congruent with the EBTs, in which there is little concrete narrative, but much abstract teaching [2] [3]. Simple lotuses appear, lacking the sophisticated design of later times.

The monument was discovered by surveying the landscape of a large area that according to a number of sources had, in ancient times, been within the sphere of Buddhist influence and where a monument would thus be expected, but had not yet been discovered [2]. That the location of monuments could be predicted in this way suggests that Buddhism was well established in this whole region by the time of Asoka.

The monument contains two *brahmī* inscriptions that appear to connect donors (of the Bahuśrutīya school) directly to the Buddha through teacher/student lineages [1, 16]. These inscriptions include Buddhist terms such as *bhagavat*, Budha, *upasaka*, *ācariya*, and *ātevāsi* (= *antevāsī*) [1]. The inscriptions are damaged and full reconstruction is not possible; however, in so far as the reconstruction allows, they go back to the Buddha in 9 to 14 generations. This shows that the Buddha was regarded as a historical person who lived a couple of centuries prior to the inscriptions. Moreover, it shows the Buddha as the originator of the lineage and therefore as the source of Buddhism.

References

[1] HINÜBER, Oskar VON and SKILLING, Peter. "Two Buddhist Inscriptions from Deorkothar". In: *Annual Report of the International Research Institute for Advanced Buddhology at Soka University (ARIRIAB)*. Vol. XVI. 2013, pp. 13–26.

[2] MISHRA, P.K. *Deokorthar: A milestone of history*. 2003. URL: http://pib.nic.in/feature/feyr2003/ffeb2003/f040220031.html.

[3] MISHRA, P.K. *Does Newly Excavated Buddhist Temple Provide A Missing Link?* 2001. URL: http://archive.archaeology.org/online/news/deorkothar/index.html.

5.6 Bhārhut

Bhārhut is a major archaeological site that attests to Buddhism as a major, well-established Indian religion from the time of Asoka.

This stupa was begun by Asoka, although most of what we can now see is dated to the Sunga dynasty in 2nd and early 1st century BCE [4, 403] [5]. It includes many Buddhist images and references. Representations of the Buddha are aniconic. Many details from the EBTs are depicted or mentioned in inscriptions, including:

1. **Buddhas:** Buddha Gotama and all five past Buddhas of the EBTs are mentioned, but none other: Sāka Muni [2, 134]; Kāsapa [2, 135]; Konigamena (= Konāgamana) [2, 132]; Vipasi [2, 137]; Vesabhu [2, 132]; Kakusadha [2, 137].

2. **People:** Ajātasatru [2, 127]; Rāja Pasenaji Kosalo (= King Pasenadi of Kosala) [2, 134]; Dighatapasi (= Dīgha Tapassī) (MN 56/MĀ 133) [6, 159–160].

3. **Places:** Kosambī [6, 7]; Pāṭaliputa [2, 139]; Sudhamma deva sabhā (= Sudhamma Hall of the Gods) (MN 50.29) [2, 136]; Vijayanto Pāsāde (= Vejayanta Palace) (MN 37.8/SĀ 505/EĀ 19.3) [2, 137]; Ida sāla guha (= Cave-hall of Indra) (DN 21.1.1) [2, 138].

4. **Scenes from the Buddha's life:** Awakening (MN 26.18/MĀ 204, MN 36.43) [4, 404]; first discourse (SN 56:11/SĀ 379/T 109/T 110/EĀ 19.2/P 747/P 1003) [4, 404]; Indra's visit (DN 21/DĀ 14/T 15/MĀ 134) [4, 404]; worship by King Ajātasattu (DN 2.99–101/DĀ 27/T 22/EĀ 43.7) [4, 404]; passing away (DN 16.6.7–9/DĀ 2/T 5/T 6/T 7/T 1451/SMPS 42.11–18) [4, 404]. Particularly interesting is a pillar that depicts and labels several scenes from the Mahāparinibbāna Sutta [3, 143]. This suggests a familiarity with this discourse, which therefore must have existed.

5. **Text reciters:** *sutantika* [2, 138]; *pamcha-nekāyika* (= *pañca-nekayika)* [6, 37].[6]

6. **Technical terms:** *amtevāsi* [6, 43]; *arāmika* [6, 168]; *avāsikā* [2, 143]; *bhatudesaka* [2, 139]; *navakamika* [6, 38] [2, 136]; *upadāna* [6, 38].

7. **Divine beings:** Ajakālako (= Ajakalāpaka) (Ud 1:7) [2, 138]; Erapato nāja rāja (= Erakapatta, king of nāgas) (AN 4:67) [2, 134–135] [6, 110–113]; Kupiro (= Kuvera; also known as Vessavana; e.g. at AN 7:53) [2, 138]; Muchalido nāgarāja (= Mucalinda, king of nāgas) (Ud 2:1) [6, 104]; Suchiloma (SN 10:3/SĀ 1324/SĀ² 323) [2, 136]; Sudhāvāsa devas [6, 97]; Vipachitta (= Vepacitti) (e.g. at SN 11:4/SĀ 1110/SĀ² 39/ EĀ 34.8) [1]; Virudako (= Virūlhaka) (DN 18.11) [2, 134].

8. **Plants:** Bodhi tree of Gotama Buddha [2, 127]; for Vesabhu this is specified as a Sal tree [2, 132], for Konāgamana as an Udumbara tree, for Kakusandha as a Sirisha tree and for Kassapa as a Nyagrodha tree, all as in DN 14.1.8 [6, 85–86]. Only the tree of Buddha Vipassī does not fit with the EBT description, which specifies the Pāṭalī tree. Instead it is given as the Asoka tree, as in the Mahāmāyūrī, a later Buddhist work [6, 83].[7]

9. **Assemblies:** Jātila Sabhā (Vin I 33) [2, 131]; deva sabhā (AN 3:37) [2, 136].

10. **Things:** Dhamma wheel (AN 4:36) [1]; Buddha's footprint (AN 4:36) [6, 104].

11. **Acts:** Frequent mention of donations (*dāna*) [2, 127*ff*].

12. **Bhikkhunīs:** Mentioned 16 times as donors [2, 132*ff*].[8]

---

[6] The words *bhānaka* [2, 140], "reciter", and *petaki* [6, 37], "knower of the *piṭaka*", are also found, implying recitation of Buddhist texts, although these terms are not found in the EBTs.

[7] For a discussion of the Mahāmāyūrī see Sørensen [7].

[8] Monks are mentioned about the same number of times, however using the less specific forms *aya* or *bhadanta* [2, 130*ff*].

Shortly after Asoka we thus find references to collections of scripture (see also section 5.7, "Sāñcī" below), to individual scriptures contained therein (see section 5.2, "Asokan edicts"), and to many people, places, ideas, and objects familiar from the EBTs. This is not just true of generalities, but also sometimes of details: according to Lüders "... the visit of Ajātasattu [to the Buddha] is depicted even in details exactly according to the Sāmaññaphala Sutta," and "... the representation of the visit of Sakka [to the Buddha] follows the text of the Sakkapañha Sutta." [6, 70] This suggests that the EBTs must have existed at this time.

There is further evidence to suggest that the EBTs were considerably earlier. Bhārhut's early detailed Buddhist images and inscriptions depict a context later than that of the EBTs and familiar from Buddhist literature such as the developed Buddha legends and non-EBT Jātakas. Since such literature inherits and builds on the EBTs, this shows that the EBTs had been extant and influential for a considerable period of time prior to Bhārhut. Such non-EBT details include:

1. **Buddha legend:** Māyā's dream, depicting the conception of the Bodhisatta as the descent of an elephant (JN 67) [1] [6, 89]; childhood contest (JN 78) [4, 404]; Prince Siddhattha leaving Kapilavatthu on his horse Kanthaka, whose feet are upheld by four Yakkhas (JN 83) [6, 93]; cutting of the Buddha-to-be's hair (JN 86) [4, 404]; worship by *pārileyyaka* elephants (Vin I 353) [4, 404]; visit of *nāga* Erakapatta[9] (Dhp-a III 234) [4, 404].

2. **Jātakas:** About 40 in all [4, 404], of which 16 are mentioned by name, while others just appear in image. Some are still unidentified [2, 130–131].

3. **Relic worship:** and stupa worship (DN 16.6.27–28/SMPS 50–51)[10] [2, plate XXXI].

4. **Purchase of Jetavana:** (Vin II 158–159; JN 125) [2, 133].

[9] Lamotte says Erāpatha, but the correct Pali spelling seems to be Erakapatta [6, 110–113].

[10] This verse, which is a late addition to the Mahāparinibbāna Sutta and acknowledged as such by the commentary, appears to be the earliest reference to relic/stupa worship.

5. **Saṅkika/Saṅkassa ladder:** The Buddha's descent from Tāvatiṁsa heaven (e.g. Dhp-a III 224) [1].

6. ***Gadhakuti* and *Kosabakuti*:** Huts/houses of the Buddha's according to non-EBT tradition (e.g. DN-a II 1 and Jātakas) [6, 107–108].

7. ***Patisamdhi*:** An Abhidhamma term that refers to rebirth [6, 87–88].

References

[1] BURDAK, L. *Bharhut*. 2007–2012. URL: http://www.jatland.com/w/index.php?title=Bharhut&oldid=169485.

[2] CUNNINGHAM, Alexander. *The Stupa of Bharhut*. 1879. URL: http://www.archive.org/stream/cu31924016181111#page/n3/mode/2up.

[3] DEHEJIA, V. *Discourse in Early Buddhist Art: Visual Narratives of India*. Munshiram Manoharlal Publishers, 1997.

[4] LAMOTTE, Étienne. *History of Indian Buddhism: From the Origins to the Śaka Era*. Publications de l'Institut orientaliste de Louvain. Université catholique de Louvain, Institut orientaliste, 1988.

[5] LÜDERS, H. *Bharhut und Die Buddhistische Literatur*. Kraus, 1966.

[6] LÜDERS, H., WALDSCHMIDT, E., and MEHENDALE, A. *Corpus Inscriptionum Indicarum: Vol. II Part II Bharhut Inscriptions*. Government epigraphist for India, 1963. URL: http://archive.org/stream/corpusinscriptio014676mbp/corpusinscriptio014676mbp_djvu.txt.

[7] SØRENSEN, Henrik H. "The Spell of the Great, Golden Peacock Queen: The Origin, Practices, and Lore of an Early Esoteric Buddhist Tradition in China". In: *Pacific World Journal*. Third 8 (2006).

5.7 Sāñcī

Sāñcī is a large complex which shows that Buddhism had spread and was powerful a long way from the Ganges plain within 150–200 years of the lifetime of the Buddha.

This monastery/stupa complex is located near Vidisa, which is nearly 1,000 km from Pāṭaliputta. It originated in Asoka's time, although, like Bhārhut, much of what we see today was added a century or so later [2, 311–312] [3, 33] [5, 363].[11]

At Sāñcī were discovered relics of the Buddha's chief disciples, Sāriputta and Moggallāna, both of whom are prominent in the EBTs. There were also smaller stupas that contained relics and references to several later monks as "teachers of the Himalayas." These monks are identical to several of the monks that according to the Sinhalese Vinaya Commentary (in Pali and Chinese) were missionaries in the time of King Asoka. This was one of the cardinal identifications that allowed scholars to conclude that the traditional accounts of Asoka contained some historical facts. Wynne has recently strengthened the case by making the point that the relics were found together in groups of five, the minimum size group required to confer ordination, thus pointing to their missionary purpose [6, 50]. He also argues that some of the Asokan Edicts refer to the same missionary activities [6, 54–59].

The Eastern Gateway of the main stupa is decorated with bas-relief that depicts Asoka sending a branch of the Bodhi tree to Sri Lanka [4, 302–303]. This event is also mentioned in RE 13 [1]. Both of these corroborate the story in the Mahāvaṁsa of the establishment of Buddhism in Sri Lanka at the time of Asoka (Mv 13.18–13.21, Mv 14.1–14.65).

References

[1] DHAMMIKA, S., trans. *The Edicts of King Asoka.* 1994–2013. URL: http://www.accesstoinsight.org/lib/authors/dhammika/wheel386.html.

[2] LAMOTTE, Étienne. *History of Indian Buddhism: From the Origins to the Śaka Era.* Publications de l'Institut orientaliste de Louvain. Université catholique de Louvain, Institut orientaliste, 1988.

[3] MARSHALL, John. *A Guide to Sanchi.* 1918. URL: http://asi.nic.in/asi_books/4365.pdf.

[4] RHYS DAVIDS, T.W. *Buddhist India.* Putnam, 1903. URL: http://fsnow.com/text/buddhist-india/.

[5] SINGH, U. *A History of Ancient and Early Medieval India: From the Stone Age to the 12th Century.* Pearson Education, 2008.

[11] The exception being the gateways, which were added around the end of the 1st century CE [3, 33].

[6] WYNNE, Alexander. "The Historical Authenticity of Early Buddhist Literature". In: *Vienna Journal of South Asian Studies* XLIX (2005), pp. 35–70. URL: http://www.ocbs.org/images/stories/awynne2005wzks.pdf.

5.7.1 Artwork

The art at Sāñcī harks back to the EBTs, even as it develops in new directions.

Although most of the artwork at Sāñcī is quite elaborate and reflects trends in the non-EBT Buddha biography, it is for the most part based on material found in the EBTs and ultimately refers back to this. As with Bhārhut, this suggests that the EBTs are the root from which this artwork sprang, but that there has been an extensive period of development and elaboration in the time after the EBTs. In the following we have referred both to the EBT root sources and the sources of the later elaboration, wherever applicable.

Most of the art at Sāñcī is concerned with the life of the Buddha. The following general development in the Buddha biography can be discerned in the scenes depicted at Sāñcī.

1. **Straight from EBTs:** Birth: lotus and standing Māyā (MN 123.15) [1, 79] [5, 48]; austerities (MN 12/T 757, MN 36.20–30, EĀ 31.8) [3, 405]; Awakening: Bodhi tree with empty seat (Vin I 1) [1, 79] [5, 44–46]; first teaching: *Dhammacakka* and deer (MN 26.29–30/MĀ 204/EĀ 24.5) [1, 78–79] [2, 278] [5, 44–46]; Bamboo Grove in Rājagaha [5, 66]; Indasālā: Sakka's visit (DN 21/DĀ 14/T 15/MĀ 134) [1, 81]; Ajātasattu's visit (DN 2.12/DĀ 27/T 22/EĀ 43.7) [3, 406]; Mahāparinibbāna: stupa (DN 16.6.7–9/DĀ 2/T 5/T 6/T 7/T 1451/SMPS 42.11–18) [1, 79] [5, 44–46]; division of relics (DN 16.6.24–27/SMPS 51.8–21) [1, 81].

2. **EBTs, with elaboration:** First meditation (MN 36.31/EĀ 31.8 and JN 77) [3, 405]; divine messengers (DN 14.2–14) [1, 79] [2, 202–203]; Brahmā and Sakka, with retinue, ask Buddha to teach (MN 26.20–21 and JN 108) [1, 80] [5, 73]; strife brewing over the Buddha's relics, "War of the Relics" (DN 16.6.25/SMPS 50) [3, 405] [5, 77].

3. **Borderline EBT:** Serpent Mucalinda (Ud 1:11/Vin I 3) [1, 80]; two first disciples, Tapussa and Bhallika (Vin I 4) [1, 80]; guardian devas

give four bowls (Vin I 4) [1, 80]; victory over *nāga* (Vin I 25) [1, 80]; Indra and Brahmā visit Buddha at Uruvelā (Vin I 26–27) [3, 405] [5, 73]; the Buddha stops splitting of wood and lighting of fire (Vin I 31) [1, 80]; parts water and walks on dry ground (Vin I 32) [1, 80] [5, 83]; visits Kapilavatthu (Vin I 82–83 and JN 118–119) [3, 405]; converts Jaṭilas [3, 405]; Bimbisāra's visit (Vin I 35–39 and JN 111–112) [2, 232] [3, 94] [5, 73]; Buddha's footprint with *dhammacakka* (AN 4:36) [5, 49].

4. **Mostly non-EBT, but with EBT kernel:** Māyā's dream, conception (MN 123.6–7/MĀ 32 and JN 67) [2, 202] [3, 405]; temptation and assault by Māra, his daughters and host of demons (Snp 3:2 and JN 95–98, 105–106) [1, 79] [5, 61]; Buddha's residences at Jetavana, and the spread of coins for buying the Jetavana (JN 125) [1, 80] [3, 405] [5, 65]; gift of Nigrodhārāma to Sangha (JN 119) [3, 405]; teaching the Sakyas (JN 119–120) [1, 80] [3, 405]; offering of honey by monkey in Pārileyyaka forest[12] (Dhp-a I 59–60) [1, 81].

5. **Non-EBT:** Buddha-to-be leaves on the horse Kanthaka (JN 83–86) [1, 79] [3, 410]; Kanthaka's legs supported by devas (JN 83) [1, 67]; Sujātā offers milk rice (JN 92) [1, 79]; Sotthiya (Svastika) offers grass to Buddha at Bodhi tree (JN 93) [1, 79]; Buddha walks meditating after Awakening (JN 104) [1, 79]; jewel house where Buddha contemplates Abhidhamma after Awakening (JN 104) [1, 79]; twin wonder under mango tree at Sāvatthī (Jā no. 483) [1, 80]; Buddha goes to Tāvatiṁsa heaven to teach Abhidhamma to mother (Dhp-a III 216) [1, 80] [3, 405]; Saṅkassa: descent from Tāvatiṁsa (e.g. Dhp-a III 224) [1, 80].

The art at Sāñcī also includes some scenes that are not from the Buddha's biography. An evolution similar to that in the Buddha biography can be seen in this art too:

1. **Straight from EBTs:** Six Buddhas and their trees (DN 14.1.8): Vipassī with *pāṭalī*, the trumpet flower tree;[13] Sikhī with *puṇḍarīka*, the white

[12] Ahir and Lamotte [3, 406] say in Vesālī, but this appears to be wrong.

[13] According to Lüders, however, the tree depicted for Vipassī is the Asoka tree, which does not accords with the EBTs but with the Mahāmāyūrī, a later Buddhist work [4, 83].

mango tree; Vessabhū with *sālā* tree; Kakusandha with *sirīsa*, the *acacia sirissa* tree; Konāgamana with *udumbara*, fig tree; Kassapa with *nigrodha*, Banyan tree; Gotama with *assattha*, the *Ficus Religiosa* [1, 82]. Cosmography: Four Great Kings, Kubera (Vessavaṇa), Virūḷhaka, Virūpakkha, and Dhataraṭṭha (e.g. DN 18.12) [5, 46]. The six *kāmāvacara* heavens (AN 3:70) [5, 69–70].

2. **Mostly non-EBT, but with EBT kernel:** Maitreya with his tree of awakening [1, 82].[14]

3. **Non-EBT:** Relic worship (DN 16.6.28/SMPS 50–51) [2, 215, 227]; Asoka visits *stupa* at Rāmagāma (Aśokāvadāna [6, 112, 219]) [1, 82]; Asoka visits Bodhi tree (RE 5 and Aśokāvadāna [6, 125–127, 250, 257]) [1, 82] [5, 54, 68]; five Jātaka stories [1, 81].

References

[1] AHIR, D.C. *Buddhist Shrines in India.* B.R. Publishing Corporation, 1986.

[2] CUNNINGHAM, Alexander. *The Bhilsa topes: or, Buddhist monuments of central India: comprising a brief historical sketch of the rise, progress, and decline of Buddhism; with an account of the opening and examination of the various groups of topes around Bhilsa.* Smith, Elder, 1854. URL: https://archive.org/details/cu31924022980571.

[3] LAMOTTE, Étienne. *History of Indian Buddhism: From the Origins to the Śaka Era.* Publications de l'Institut orientaliste de Louvain. Université catholique de Louvain, Institut orientaliste, 1988.

[4] LÜDERS, H., WALDSCHMIDT, E., and MEHENDALE, A. *Corpus Inscriptionum Indicarum: Vol. II Part II Bharhut Inscriptions.* Government epigraphist for India, 1963. URL: http://archive.org/stream/corpusinscriptio014676mbp/corpusinscriptio014676mbp_djvu.txt.

[5] MARSHALL, John. *A Guide to Sanchi.* 1918. URL: http://asi.nic.in/asi_books/4365.pdf.

[6] STRONG, J.S., trans. *The Legend of King Aśoka: A Study and Translation of the Aśokāvadāna.* Buddhist tradition. Motilal Banarsidass, 1989.

[14] Thus all seven Buddhas of the EBTs are depicted at Sāñcī, but none other.

5.7.2 Inscriptions

The inscriptions at Sañcī, though modest in quantity, use terms and ideas from the EBTs.

There are few inscriptions at Sāñcī compared to Bhārhut. Still, the few inscriptions that are found there include a number of terms that either refer to the EBTs or include vocabulary which has the EBTs as its source.

1. **Reciters of scriptural collections:** *sutātika* [2, 150], *sutātikinī* [2, 150], *sūtātikinī* [2, 150],[15] *dhamakathika* [2, 414], *pacenekayika* (= *pañcanekāyika*) [1, 254], *sutatikiniyā* [1, 257].

2. **Technical terms:** *āchariya* [1, 287], *anantarya*[16] [2, 415], *antevāsi* [1, 247, 254–255, 280, 282, 288], *araha* (= *arahant*) [1, 250, 257–258], *ārya-Sangha* [4, 37], *bhagavat* [1, 241], *bhikhu* [1, 236–240, 243, 246–247, 252–256, 280–281, 283–284], *bhikhuni* [1, 235–239, 245–246, 249, 252, 254–255, 257–258, 281–284], *budha* [1, 245], *chilathitika* [1, 260–261], *dhama* [1, 246] [2, 412], nikāya [1, 239], *sadhivihārī* [2, 414], *samaga* [1, 261], *samanera* [1, 238, 253], *sagha* (= *sangha*) [1, 251, 261], *saghadana* (= *sanghadāna*) [1, 249], *sapurisa* [1, 255, 287–289] [3, 3], *thera* [2, 414] [3, 3], *upāsikā* [1, 240, 243, 251] [4, 37], *upāsaka* [3, 2], *vināyaka* [1, 286] [3, 3], *vinayakāna* [1, 286].

3. **Names:** Sāriputa (relics) [1, 297], Mahā Mogalāna (relics) [1, 297], Idadeva (= Sakka) [2, 412].

References

[1] CUNNINGHAM, Alexander. *The Bhilsa topes: or, Buddhist monuments of central India: comprising a brief historical sketch of the rise, progress, and decline of Buddhism; with an account of the opening and examination of the various groups of topes around Bhilsa*. Smith, Elder, 1854. URL: https://archive.org/details/cu31924022980571.

[15] It is not entirely clear from Lamotte's text where these there terms are found, but it would seem they are either from Bhārut or Sāñcī.

[16] A term for karma that ripens immediately.

[2] LAMOTTE, Étienne. *History of Indian Buddhism: From the Origins to the Śaka Era.* Publications de l'Institut orientaliste de Louvain. Université catholique de Louvain, Institut orientaliste, 1988.

[3] LÜDERS, H., WALDSCHMIDT, E., and MEHENDALE, A. *Corpus Inscriptionum Indicarum: Vol. II Part II Bharhut Inscriptions.* Government epigraphist for India, 1963. URL: http://archive.org/stream/corpusinscriptio014676mbp/corpusinscriptio014676mbp_djvu.txt.

[4] MARSHALL, John. *A Guide to Sanchi.* 1918. URL: http://asi.nic.in/asi_books/4365.pdf.

5.8 Piprahwa/Ganwaria

The Piprahwa finds appear to include genuine relics from the Buddha's cremation, thus lending support to the historical reliability of the Mahāparinibbāna Sutta and by implication the EBTs as a whole.

A soapstone casket (the "Peppé casket") with Asokan Brahmi inscriptions, apparently containing relics of the Buddha, was discovered in a large stupa at Piprahwa towards the end of the nineteenth century [5, 78]. The inscription, as well as the location of the find, implies that the Sakyas received some of the relics of the Buddha after his cremation and that the Sakyans belonged to this area [2, 156].[17] This echoes the distribution of relics described at the end of the Mahāparinibbāna Sutta (DN 16.6.24–26/ SMPS 51.9–21). The exact interpretation of the inscription is disputed [3, 140], but it seems likely it should be understood as follows:

> "This receptacle for the relics of the Blessed Buddha is that of the Sakyan brothers called Suki, together with their wives and children."
>
> *Sukiti bhatinaṁ sa-puta-dalanaṁ iyam salila-nidhane Budhasa bhagavate sakiyānaṁ.* [4, 103]

Further excavations revealed another relic casket at a lower level than the Peppé casket, once again with bone relics, but without inscription,

[17] The discovery has proved controversial since it is tied up with the identification of ancient Kapilavatthu. Two different sites, Piprahwa in India and Tilaurakot in Nepal, have been identified as the possible location of Kapilavatthu. If the find at Piprahwa is genuine, as attested by as one of the world's leading epigraphists, Prof. Harry Falk, [1] this will significantly strengthen its claim to be the site of ancient Kapilavatthu.

and dated to the Mauryan period [2, 157]. Excavations a few hundred metres from the stupa yielded a number of sealings with the inscription *Kapilavastu* [4, 106]. This discovery substantially strengthens the case that the Piprahwa find is linked to the relic distribution described in the Mahāparinibbāna Sutta.

The earliest archaeological finds of Piprahwa and the nearby site of Ganwaria, such as the mud walls closest to the natural soil level, probably date to around 500 BCE [2, 159], again consonant with the dates of the Buddha and descriptions in the EBTs.

References

[1] ALLEN, Charles and FALK, Harry. *The Bones of the Buddha—an expert opinion on the Piprahwa Stupa.* 2013. URL: http://www.youtube.com/watch?v=HwhABtpl5Q8.

[2] HÄRTEL, Herbert. "Archaeological Research on Ancient Buddhist Sites". In: *When Did the Buddha Live?: The Controversy on the Dating of the Historical Buddha.* Bibliotheca Indo-Buddhica. Sri Satguru, 1995.

[3] SALOMON, Richard. *Indian Epigraphy: A Guide to the Study of Inscriptions in Sanskrit, Prakrit, and the other Indo-Aryan Languages.* South Asia Research. Oxford University Press, USA, 1998.

[4] SRIVASTAVA, K.M. "Archaeological Excavations at Piprāhwā and Ganwaria and the Identification of Kapilavastu". In: *Journal of the International Association of Buddhist Studies* 3.1 (1980), pp. 103–110.

[5] SRIVASTAVA, K.M. *Buddha's Relics from Kapilavastu.* Agam Kala Prakashan, 1986.

5.9 Rājagaha

Rājagaha's striking geography is depicted in many places in the EBTs, and the Buddhist presence is confirmed by many archaeological sites.

The hills around Rājagaha feature in the EBTs, and the striking geography inspired several discourses, similes, and stories. The hot springs, which were the occasion for a Vinaya rule, are still present. Many ruins of stupas and monasteries are found, although it is difficult to know what period they may be traced back to.

There is a cave that has been identified with the Sattapaṇṇi Cave, in which the First Council was held; if this is correct, the Council must have been a humble affair, for the cave is small.

The hills feature a dry-stone wall some 40 kilometres long, the remnant of ancient fortifications. These are probably pre-Mauryan, from the time when Rājagaha was still the main city of Magadha. The EBTs mention that king Ajātasattu was fortifying Rājagaha soon after the Buddha had died (MN 108/MĀ 145) [2, 48–49]. This may be equivalent to the wall from New Rājagaha, which has been firmly dated to the 4th century BCE, thus matching closely with the information given in the EBTs [1, 145].

References

[1] HÄRTEL, Herbert. "Archaeological Research on Ancient Buddhist Sites". In: *When Did the Buddha Live?: The Controversy on the Dating of the Historical Buddha*. Bibliotheca Indo-Buddhica. Sri Satguru, 1995.

[2] TADDEI, M. *The Ancient Civilization of India*. Barrie and Jenkins, 1970.

5.10 Mathurā

The city of Mathurā has a rich archaeology, the details of which agree with its depiction in the EBTs.

Mathurā appears in the archaeological record as a major centre of Buddhism from around 150 BCE [1, 1]. The stone artwork has a characteristic "Mathuran" style, which suggests a period of development in perishable materials during an earlier unattested artistic culture [1]. Prior to this we have some traces of mud brick walls from the 3rd century BCE, and earlier than that only some Northern Black Polished Ware, terracotta, and metal items [1, 1]. In the time of the Buddha, therefore, Mathurā was probably a minor trading town.[18]

This agrees with the depiction of Mathurā in the EBTs, where Mathurā is described as having five drawbacks: the ground is uneven, there is a lot

[18] In AN 4:53 the Buddha is said to be traveling between Madurā and Verañja, presumably following the trade route to the north-west.

of dust, the dogs are fierce, there are evil *yakkhas* and it is difficult to get alms food (AN 5:220).

The growth of Mathurā from a dusty town to a prosperous city agrees with MN 84 and AN 2:38, which are set after the time of the Buddha. The mention of a king, and the concern with winning over the ruling class of Mathurā, suggest the growing importance of Mathurā as Buddhism spread to the north-west.

References

[1] QUINTANILLA, S.R. *History of Early Stone Sculpture at Mathura, ca. 150 BCE–100 CE*. Studies in Asian Art and Archaeology. Brill.

5.11 Other Mauryan excavations

Many other excavations have confirmed the existence, around the lifetime of the Buddha, of places that are mentioned in the EBTs.

In addition to the above, Asokan era Buddhist remains have been discovered at all of the most important locations mentioned in the EBTs, and also at many lesser locations, such as: Kapilavatthu[19] (MN 14.1/MĀ 100/T 54/T 55) [2, 150] [3, 320]; Kosambī (SN 22:81/SĀ 973/SĀ² 207) [2, 146–147] [3, 322–324]; Kusinārā (DN 16.5.1/SMPS 32.4) [3, 319]; Lumbinī [2, 149–150]; Nāḷandā (DN 1.1.1) [3, 322]; Pāṭaligāma/Pāṭaliputta/Patna (DN 16.1.19/SMPS 4.2) [3, 321–322]; Pāvā (DN 29.1) [3, 319–320]; Rāmagāma (DN 16.6.24/SMPS 51.13) [3, 315]; Sārnāth (SN 56:11)[20] [2, 145] [3, 317]; Sāvatthī, including the Jetavana (e.g. MN 4.1/EĀ 31.1) [2, 147–148] [3, 321]; and Vesālī (e.g. MN 12.1/T 757) [2, 148–149] [3, 321].

At Sāvatthī archaeological excavations have established that the ancient town goes back at least to the middle of the 6th century BCE [2, 148]. Regarding Vesālī, Härtel dates the earliest habitation to around 500 BCE [2, 149].

At Kosambī a stone slab from the Kuṣāṇa period (1st–3rd century CE) with the inscription Ghositārāma Vihāra links this find to the EBTs [2,

[19] The general area is agreed on, but two possible locations have been identified.
[20] Here called Isipatana.

146]. Archaeological excavations at Kosambī have unearthed fortifications dating to as early as the 6th century BCE [2, 147]. Again, this fits with the dating of the Buddha to the 5th century BCE and the mention of Kosambī in the EBTs.

In general, there is a remarkable correspondence between the archaeological record and the main towns of the middle Ganges plain as described in the EBTs. Bronkhorst says [1, 4, note 10]: "Erdosy recalls that Buddhist tradition recognizes six cities of outstanding importance which would have been fit to receive the mortal remains of the Buddha—Campā, Kāśī, Śrāvastī, Kauśāmbī, Rājagṛha and Sāketa—and points out that the first five of these correspond to the earliest urban centres reconstructed from archaeological evidence, omitting only Ujjain."

References

[1] BRONKHORST, Johannes. *Greater Magadha: studies in the culture of early India.* Brill, 2007.

[2] HÄRTEL, Herbert. "Archaeological Research on Ancient Buddhist Sites". In: *When Did the Buddha Live?: The Controversy on the Dating of the Historical Buddha.* Bibliotheca Indo-Buddhica. Sri Satguru, 1995.

[3] LAMOTTE, Étienne. *History of Indian Buddhism: From the Origins to the Śaka Era.* Publications de l'Institut orientaliste de Louvain. Université catholique de Louvain, Institut orientaliste, 1988.

5.12 South Indian art and inscriptions

The archaeology of South India confirms the spread of Buddhism and Aryan culture subsequent to the Asokan period.

Amarāvatī, a major Buddhist site in Andhra Pradesh, attests to the spread of Buddhism to the south shortly after Asoka. It has been estimated that the earliest Buddhist art at Amarāvatī stems from the second or even third century BCE [1, 105–108]. It shares the aniconic features and workmanship of early North Indian Buddhist art [2, 345, 403].

According to the Chinese pilgrim Xuan Zang, who visited South India in the 7th century, there was a monastery built by Mahinda, Asokas's son, in the Pandyan country, which is close to Sri Lanka [3, 49–50]. Thus there is an ancient tradition that Buddhism arrived in South India in the Asokan period.

The fact that Buddhism was well-established in the south of India at such an early period attests to a movement that had already been in existence for a considerable period of time.

References

[1] KARLSSON, Klemens. *Face to Face with the Absent Buddha. The Formation of Buddhist Aniconic Art*. Uppsala University, 1999. URL: http://www.diva-portal.org/smash/get/diva2:164388/FULLTEXT01.pdf.

[2] LAMOTTE, Étienne. *History of Indian Buddhism: From the Origins to the Śaka Era*. Publications de l'Institut orientaliste de Louvain. Université catholique de Louvain, Institut orientaliste, 1988.

[3] SMITH, V.A. *Asoka: The Buddhist Emperor of India*. Rulers of India. Kessinger Publishing, 2006.

5.13 Northern Black Polished Ware culture

The culture characterised by pottery known as Northern Black Polished Ware (NBPW) spans the same region at the same time as the EBTs.

The sparse archaeological finds in the period from around 500 BCE to the Mauryan era are characterised as the Northern Black Polished Ware (NBPW) culture, named after the glazed pottery common to this era [1, 141 and note 2]. The cultural complex of this time also includes iron and the gradual introduction of burnt brick and coinage.

It is likely that Magadha's rise to power was connected to iron ore mines south of Rājagaha, the iron from which could be used for weapons and tools. The furnaces used to prepare the iron may have been instrumental in the production of NBPW [2] [3, 171]; at the very least the simultaneous appearance of iron and new forms of pottery attest to a development in the control of fire. The use of iron is widely attested in the EBTs and, to a lesser extent, also the use of coins. Burnt bricks, however, are only attested in the *vibhaṅga* and Khandhakas of the Vinaya,[21] which are generally later than the EBTs.[22]

The geographical distribution of the NBPW culture is, apart from the outlier of Amarāvatī, similar to the geographical area known to the EBTs, although the NBPW culture is found over a slightly wider area due to its prevalence until the Asokan period.[23] This confirms that, despite the political divisions, this region was a relatively unified culture in this period, which again is consonant with the EBTs.

The small scale and low level of urbanisation found in the NBPW culture also agree with the EBTs, which do not contain descriptions of large cities.

References

[1] HÄRTEL, Herbert. "Archaeological Research on Ancient Buddhist Sites". In: *When Did the Buddha Live?: The Controversy on the Dating of the Historical Buddha*. Bibliotheca Indo-Buddhica. Sri Satguru, 1995.

[2] SHARMA, H. *Short notes on Northern Black Polished Ware (NBP)*. 2012. URL: http://www.preservearticles.com/2012012721730/short-notes-on-northern-black-polished-ware-nbp.html.

[3] SIMSON, Georg von. "The historical background of the rise of Buddhism and the problem of dating". In: *When Did the Buddha Live?: The Controversy on the Dating of the Historical Buddha*. Bibliotheca Indo-Buddhica. Sri Satguru, 1995.

---

21 Vin II 120,35; Vin II 121,4; Vin II 152,9–11; Vin II 159,33; Vin III 81,12–13; Vin IV 266,5.

22 See section 3.1.3, "Later borrowing", above.

23 It was the great social and technological changes under the Mauryan Empire, including the introduction of substantial trade with the West, that marked the end of the NBPW culture.

CHAPTER 6

Development of Buddhism

Changes in Buddhism can be traced in many areas, over a long period, and show a consistent arc of development that is consistent with the kinds of developments seen in other religions.

Earlier and later texts can be distinguished because the later ones contain developments not found in the earlier texts. At the same time the later texts refer to the earlier texts and assume their existence. Without the earlier texts the later ones do not make sense, whereas the EBTs are independent of later developments.

6.1 First Council

All early schools for which records are still available have a memory of how the EBTs were recited and systematised soon after the Buddha's passing away.

The First Council is recorded in the Vinaya of all schools whose texts are available [2, 129, 150] [3, 100, 173–174]. While they differ on details, each implying that it was their own version of the canon that was recited [2, 150], they all agree that the business of the council was to recite the EBTs. These Vinaya accounts of the first Council all contain details about which Suttas and which parts of the Vinaya were recited, showing that the EBTs existed in some form in all these schools [6].

Certain Vinayas—the Dharmaguptaka, the Sarvāstivāda, the Mūlasarvāstivāda, and the Vinayamātṛkā Sūtra—also add the Abhidhamma, although the Pali, Mahāsāṅghika, and Mahīśāsaka Vinayas notably omit any mention of the Abhidhamma [2, 151].[1]

This is significant, as the Abhidhamma was a vital part of Theravādin self-identity, and, despite this omission, later generations came to accept that it was spoken by the Buddha. Rather than make a simple addition to their canonical text, the Theravādins preferred to authenticate the Abhidhamma through a legend of the Buddha visiting his mother in heaven and teaching her there [1, 27–28].[2] They also used the simple expedient of including the Abhidhamma in the flexible and expanding content of the Khuddaka Nikāya.[3] Thus they developed and expanded their understanding of the Buddha's teachings, but through interpretation and later legends, not by altering the EBTs.[4]

References

[1] ANĀLAYO. "Teaching the Abhidharma in the Heaven of the Thirty-three, The Buddha and his Mother". In: *Journal of the Oxford Centre for Buddhist Studies* 2 (2012), pp. 9–35.

[2] FRAUWALLNER, E. *The Earliest Vinaya and the Beginnings of Buddhist Literature.* Serie Orientale Roma. Istituto Italiano per il Medio ed Estremo Oriente, 1956.

[3] GOMBRICH, Richard. *What the Buddha Thought.* Oxford Centre for Buddhist Studies monographs. Equinox, 2009.

[4] NORMAN, K.R. *Pali Literature, Including the Canonical Literature in Prakrit and Sanskrit of all the Hinayana Schools of Buddhism.* Otto Harrassowitz, 1983.

1 A passage in the Buddha-parinirvāna Sūtra (T vol.1, no. 5, translated by Po Fa-tsu around 290–307 BCE) not only omits any mention of the Abhidhamma, but also mentions four Āgamas, against five in all the other recensions. This could point to a very early date for this passage [5, 19].

2 Analāyo makes the point that it is only in the Theravādin version of this story that the Buddha taught the Abhidhamma. In other versions he taught the Dhamma [1, 27]. Moreover, the story itself is not found in the EBTs, nor in the canonical Abhidhamma.

3 The commentaries record the opinion that the Abhidhamma is included in the Khuddaka, and also that the Khuddaka is included in the Abhidhamma, as well as a variety of other views (DN-a I 23).

4 Although the word *abhidhamma* does occasionally occur in the EBTs, it is agreed by scholars that this is not a reference to the Abhidhamma Piṭaka [4, 97].

[5] PACHOW, W. *A Comparative Study of the Pratimoksha: On the Basis of its Chinese, Tibetan, Sanskrit and Pali Versions.* Motilal Banarsidass, 2000.

[6] SUZUKI, Teitaro. "The First Buddhist Council". In: *The Monist* XIV (1904). URL: http://www.sacred-texts.com/journals/mon/1stbudcn.htm.

6.2 Second Council

A century after the Buddha there was a Second Council, also attested in all Vinayas, which confirms that the community had remained united and underlines the conservative attitude towards the teachings.

The second council, 100 years after the *parinibbāna*, was convened to decide whether certain practices taken up by certain bhikkhus were in line with the Vinaya. Most of these practices were of minor or dubious importance, while at least one had major ramifications.[5] The Sangha was in crisis, and monks gathered from a large part of Northern India to ensure the new practices were rejected [1, 131–140] [2, 22–29].

This illustrates the conservative nature of the early Sangha. Their duty, as expressed countless times, was to ensure that "the True Dhamma last long" (DN 29.17). Unlike modern academia, where innovation is rewarded, the monks were expected to hand down the teachings intact, and even minor changes or variant interpretations were considered unacceptable [3]. Moreover, there was no leader who had the authority to make such changes.[6]

A common understanding of the teachings, at least while Buddhism was still confined to a relatively small area, was promoted by monks travelling and mixing with monks from different regions.

---

5 This concerned whether monks were allowed to handle money or not.

6 MN 108.7–10 (cf. MĀ 145): "There is no single bhikkhu, brahmin, who was appointed by the Blessed One who knows and sees, accomplished and fully enlightened, thus: 'He will be your refuge when I am gone,' and whom we now have recourse to. ...There is no single bhikkhu, brahmin, who has been chosen by the Sangha and appointed by a number of elder bhikkhus thus: 'He will be our refuge after the Blessed One has gone,' and whom we now have recourse to." DN 16.6.1 (cf. SMPS 41.1–2): "Ānanda, it may be that you will think: 'The Teacher's instruction has ceased, now we have no teacher!' It should not be seen like this, Ānanda, for what I have taught and explained to you as Dhamma and discipline will, at my passing, be your teacher."

References

[1] LAMOTTE, Étienne. *History of Indian Buddhism: From the Origins to the Śaka Era*. Publications de l'Institut orientaliste de Louvain. Université catholique de Louvain, Institut orientaliste, 1988.

[2] PACHOW, W. *A Comparative Study of the Pratimoksha: On the Basis of its Chinese, Tibetan, Sanskrit and Pali Versions*. Motilal Banarsidass, 2000.

[3] WYNNE, Alexander. "The Oral Transmission of the Early Buddhist Literature". In: *Journal of the International Association of Buddhist Studies* 27.1 (2004), pp. 97–127. URL: http://archiv.ub.uni-heidelberg.de/ojs/index.php/jiabs/article/view/8945/2838.

6.3 Literary developments

The content of the later canonical books reflect the concerns of Buddhists in the Mauryan period, and it departs drastically from the EBTs.

Two trends in Buddhism in the Mauryan period were particularly influential on Buddhist literature. On the one hand, the Sangha became much larger, better endowed, and more specialised, with detailed systems of Buddhist exegesis. On the other hand, the Dhamma reached out to a much broader spectrum of the lay community.

These trends correspond to the developments of the content in the doctrinally secondary books of the early canons. On the one hand, Buddhist literature saw the evolution of the Abhidhamma texts,[7] a highly abstruse and specialised literature. On the other hand, there was the development of the popular stories of the Jātakas, Vimānavatthu, Buddha biography, and the like. This literature is thus situated naturally within the Mauryan period, and is quite unlike the literature of the EBTs, on which it depends.

Within the Pali school, the literary style of texts composed in Sri Lanka, such as the commentaries and the chronicles, is substantially different from the style of texts inherited from India [3, 175]. And since the new style that emerged in Sri Lanka is not encountered in the EBTs, it would appear that the Pali EBTs were considered closed upon their arrival on the island, that is, at the time of Asoka [3, 175–176].

[7] Including Abhidhamma style texts such as the Paṭisambhidāmagga and the Niddesa.

Also the absence of any mention in the EBTs of the Buddha visiting Sri Lanka is significant. This legend, found in several early non-EBT sources,[8] is an important part of the Sri Lankan sense of identity and it would have been tempting to slip it into the Pali EBTs. That this was not done again testifies to the conservatism of the tradition.

As for Mahāyāna texts, although the texts themselves tell us that they were spoken by the Buddha, they clearly belong to a later literary period than the EBTs. This is clear for both stylistic and linguistic reasons, and is agreed on by most Buddhist academics [1, 165] [2, 265] [4, 5].

References

[1] GOMBRICH, Richard. *What the Buddha Thought*. Oxford Centre for Buddhist Studies monographs. Equinox, 2009.

[2] MCMAHAN, David. "Orality, Writing, and Authority in South Asian Buddhism: Visionary Literature and the Struggle for Legitimacy in the Mahāyāna". In: *History of Religions* 37 (1998), pp. 249–274. URL: http://ccbs.ntu.edu.tw/FULLTEXT/JR-EPT/mc.htm.

[3] RHYS DAVIDS, T.W. *Buddhist India*. Putnam, 1903. URL: http://fsnow.com/text/buddhist-india/.

[4] WARDER, A.K. *Indian Buddhism*. Buddhism Series. Motilal Banarsidass, 2000.

6.3.1 Jātakas

The Jātaka literature is attested in the Mauryan period, yet it is clearly later than the EBTs.

Jātakas are depicted in several of the earliest Buddhist monuments, such as Bhārhut and Sāñcī, but they are clearly later than the EBTs [1, 26–28]. This is despite the fact that they often depict social conditions that are earlier than the time of the Buddha (e.g. the king in Benares) and many of them must have their roots in that period [2, 202]. The large number of Jātakas originated over a long period, some being pre-Buddhist, and were adopted into Buddhism as it became a popular religion in the Mauryan and following eras. Important developments include:

[8] It is found at Dīpavaṁsa 1–2, Mv 1, and Vin-a I 89.

1. The Jātakas, unlike the EBTs, are almost entirely narrative.
2. Even the earliest layer of the Jātakas, the verses, generally lack the distinct Buddhist terminology and doctrinal terms found in the EBTs.
3. Whereas in the EBTs the Buddha or one of his chief disciples invariably is the protagonist, in the Jātakas the protagonist is always the *bodhisatta*.
4. The structure of the Jātaka tales is different from Suttas of the EBTs [2, ch. 11].
5. The Jātakas mention things not found in the EBTs such as bricks (*iṭṭhaka*) and trade routes to countries outside of India (e.g. Jā no. 339).

References

[1] OLDENBERG, H. "The Prose-and-Verse Type of Narrative and the Jātakas". In: *Journal of the Pali Text Society* VI (1908–12), pp. 19–50.

[2] RHYS DAVIDS, T.W. *Buddhist India*. Putnam, 1903. URL: http://fsnow.com/text/buddhist-india/.

6.4 Doctrinal developments

Virtually every significant doctrine undergoes development from the time of the EBTs to the later canonical texts and beyond.

There are numerous doctrinal developments between the EBTs and non-EBTs. Such developments are not occasional or arbitrary, but follow broad-based patterns that are characteristic of philosophical and doctrinal development. This development is thoroughgoing and it is possible to pick virtually any significant teaching found in the EBTs and show how it gradually develops and evolves through the later literature. Whether such changes are merely rewordings and clarifications, or whether they indicate a genuine shift in the doctrine, is irrelevant for this point. The wording of the teachings definitely changed, and this is enough to establish the relative chronology. Some specific examples are:

1. Karma as destiny (Vimāna- and Peta-vatthu);[9]
2. Transference of merit (Petavatthu [2, XXIX, XXXVIII–XL]);[10]
3. Elaboration on and fascination with good and bad destinations of rebirth (Vimāna- and Peta-vatthu);
4. Shift in attitude to *jhāna*, especially the Abhidhammic concept of *lokuttarajjhāna* (Vibh);
5. Dependent origination happening on an 'occasion' (Vibh 145);
6. Emphasis on and detailed explanation of obscure doctrines in the EBTs, e.g. the relay coaches of MN 24/MĀ 9/EĀ 39.10 and the *kasiṇas* (Vism);
7. Increased detail and expansion in the exposition of core teachings of the EBTs, such as the description of insight (Vism);
8. Abstract teachings as opposed to applied (Abhidhamma, Paṭisambhidāmagga);
9. Systematisation of "*dhammas*" (Dhammasaṅgaṇī);
10. The explanation of dhammas as "bearing their own essence", *sabhāva* (As 39,11);
11. *Khaṇikavāda*, "doctrine of momentariness" (e.g. Vism 268,14; Vibh-a 27,3);
12. Systematisation of "conditions" (Paṭṭhāna);
13. Omniscience of the Buddha (JN 99);
14. Lineage of past Buddhas (Buddhavaṁsa);

---

9 There is some variety in the stories of the Vimāna- and Peta-vatthu, but a large number of them give a single act of charity, or the lack thereof, as the respective causes for either a splendid or a miserable rebirth [1, VII]. In the EBTs the workings of karma are much more complex. See also [2, XXVIII]

10 There are isolated mentions in EBTs, but it only becomes widespread in later Buddhism, including in inscriptions from the 1st century BCE [3, 5–7].

15. *Pāramīs* (Cariyāpiṭaka);
16. Bodhisatta path (Cariyāpiṭaka and commentaries);
17. Books on history (Aśokāvadāna, Dīpavaṁsa, Mahāvaṁsa).

Texts such as the Vibhaṅga of the Abhidhamma make it particularly clear what was the direction of these developments. The Vibhaṅga is divided into two parts: an analysis according to the Suttas and one according to the Abhidhamma. The Sutta analysis is similar to the EBTs, whereas the Abhidhamma analysis is a new development.[11] Since the Sutta material forms part of the Abhidhamma but the Abhidhamma material is not, or very rarely, found in the Suttas, the direction of development is unambiguous.

In general, the direction of doctrinal development is obvious. The texts containing new doctrines always look back to the EBTs as their starting point. This is very clear with the commentarial literature, but also with such works as the Visuddhimagga, which quotes extensively from the Suttas. The same is true of the Abhidhamma. For most non-EBT texts it can easily be shown that they base their philosophy on the EBT material but take it further, sometimes in new directions. The EBTs, by contrast, do not refer to ideas that are developed in other Buddhist literature.

References

[1] MASEFIELD, Peter, trans. *Peta stories*. Vol. XXXIV. Sacred Books of the Buddhists. The Pali Text Society, 1980.

[2] MASEFIELD, Peter, trans. *Vimāna stories*. The Pali Text Society, 1989.

[3] SCHOPEN, Gregory. *Bones, Stones, and Buddhist Monks*. University of Hawai'i Press, 1997.

6.4.1 Absence of sectarian views

Thousands of EBTs have been analysed by modern scholars to discern sectarian ideas, but such traces are very few and faint, indicating that the EBTs were essentially fixed before the sectarian period.

[11] See section 4.2.2, "Vocabulary".

There are extremely few examples of definitively sectarian views in the EBTs. One rare exception is the occasional interpolation of the three times (past, present, and future) in the Sarvāstivāda Saṁyukta Āgama [3, 72]. This means that the schools generally did not insert their own views into the EBTs, but developed them in other literature, such as the Abhidhamma [1, 875] [2, 2, 15–16].

References

[1] ANĀLAYO. *A Comparative Study of the Majjhima-nikāya*. Dharma Drum Academic Publisher, 2011.

[2] ANĀLAYO. "The Chinese Madhyama-āgama and the Pāli Majjhima-Nikāya—In the Footsteps of Thích Minh Châu". In: *The Indian International Journal of Buddhist Studies* 9 (2008). URL: http://www.buddhismuskunde.uni-hamburg.de/fileadmin/pdf/An%C4%81layo/ChineseMAPaliMN.pdf.

[3] CHOONG, Mun-keat. *The Fundamental Teachings of Early Buddhism: A Comparative Study Based on the Sūtrāṅga Portion of the Pali Saṁyutta-Nikāya and the Chinese Saṁyuktāgama*. Harrassowitz, 2000.

6.4.2 Early Abhidhamma

The Abhidhamma, which originated in the pre-sectarian period, became a separate class of literature, which shows that the EBTs were already in a developed, widely accepted, and canonical state.

The earliest stratum of Abhidhamma literature has been identified by Frauwallner, Warder, and others, on the grounds of doctrine, style, and agreement between schools [1, 14, 17, 20, 43, 45, 122, 124] [2]. This literature consists of texts that quote from the Suttas and then offer analysis or elaboration of those texts.[12] In some places they actually say they are analysing in accordance with the Suttas, as contrasted with the analysis according to the Abhidhamma.[13] But even in cases where it follows the Sutta method, the analysis involves a more developed, systematic mode

[12] The Vibhaṅga, Dharmaskandha, and Śāriputrabhidharma are based on the Saṁyutta/Saṁyukta; the Puggalapaññatti on the Aṅguttara; and the Saṅgītipariyāya on the Saṅgīti Sutta.

[13] E.g. the Vibhaṅga's Suttantabhājanīya vs. Abhidhammabhājanīya.

of analysis compared with the EBTs, though little overt change in the doctrine.[14]

The fact that these texts contain both EBT material (or very close) and new Abhidhamma material, whereas the EBTs have very few traces of Abhidhamma material, shows the direction of the development: the Abhidhamma must have come into existence after the EBTs.

Further, since some of the Abhidhamma material is shared between schools and some is not, the Abhidhamma project must have begun in the nascent sectarian period (around 300 BCE). The origin of the shared material would be even earlier, which means the EBTs must have existed before then. But even in the shared basis of these texts, the level of agreement is far less than between parallel versions of the EBTs.

References

[1] FRAUWALLNER, E., KIDD, S.F., and STEINKELLNER, E. *Studies in Abhidharma Literature and the Origins of Buddhist Philosophical Systems.* SUNY Series in Indian Thought. State University of New York Press, 1995.

[2] WARDER, A.K. *Indian Buddhism.* Buddhism Series. Motilal Banarsidass, 2000.

6.4.3 Kathāvatthu

The Kathāvatthu originated in the Mauryan period, and it extensively refers to the EBTs as canonical texts accepted by all Buddhists.

The Kathāvatthu of the Pali Abhidhamma was begun in the time of Asoka, or not long thereafter, which places its beginnings around 150–200 years after the Buddha. This dating is based on multiple lines of evidence:

1. The traditional account, which states that it was composed under Asoka [6, 7].

2. The traces of Māgadhan dialect, which are more numerous in the early sections [7, 59–70].

3. The agreement with the Vijñānakāya, a similar but much briefer analysis in Sanskrit [4, 86]. This mentions the Kathāvatthu's author

[14] See section 4.2.2, "Vocabulary".

by name [3, 27]. Thus the Kathāvatthu must have been started before the Sangha's dispersal to Sri Lanka and Northern India.

4. The focus on the fundamental schismatic issues, which were the hot topics of the time. Later additions to the Kathāvatthu address later issues. The Mahāyāna is never mentioned [3, 27].

The Kathāvatthu is in the form of a dialogue where the texts and ideas of the EBTs are presented and opposing interpretations given. For the Kathāvatthu, the EBTs, or more precisely the four main Nikāyas/Āgamas plus a small part of the Khuddaka Nikāya, are always the final authority in settling opposing views, not the Abhidhamma or any other Buddhist text [8, XI–XII]. In fact it argues about practically everything except the actual letter of the text of the EBTs.

It must have taken considerable time to develop such systematic doctrinal readings of the EBTs, and even longer to develop the Kathāvatthu's formal logic, which is the first example of rigorously applied formal logic in India. So the EBTs must be much earlier than this.

In several cases the Kathāvatthu quotes from EBT passages that contradict or appear to contradict the teachings of the Theravādin school itself.[15] Nevertheless, there is never any question of whether these passages might not be the word of the Buddha. In other cases, passages from the EBTs that were used by non-Theravādins in support of their special interpretations, but were awkward from a Theravādin point of view, were left untouched.[16] The disagreements are on the interpretation, not on the contents of the EBTs.

References

[1] BODHI, Bhikkhu, trans. *The Connected Discourses of the Buddha: A New Translation of the Saṁyutta Nikāya.* Teachings of the Buddha. Wisdom Publications, 2000.

[15] *Antarabhava*, AN 7:55 vs. Kv 8.2 [5, 98–108].

[16] The Puggalavādins relied on the Bhāra Sutta (SN 22:22/SĀ 73/EĀ 25.4) to bolster their argument that there is a "person" apart from the five *khandhas* [1, 1051, note 37] [2, 103, 147]. This view of the Puggalavādins is rebutted at length in the Kathāvatthu, (Kv 1.1).

[2] CHÂU, Thích Thien. *The Literature of the Personalists of Early Buddhism*. Buddhist Tradition Series. Motital Banarsidass, 2009.

[3] COUSINS, Lance. "The 'Five Points' and the origins of the Buddhist schools". In: *The Buddhist Forum: Seminar Papers 1988–1990*. Taylor & Francis, 1991.

[4] FRAUWALLNER, E., KIDD, S.F., and STEINKELLNER, E. *Studies in Abhidharma Literature and the Origins of Buddhist Philosophical Systems*. SUNY Series in Indian Thought. State University of New York Press, 1995.

[5] HARVEY, Peter. *The Selfless mind: Personality, Consciousness, and Nirvāṇa in Early Buddhism*. Curzon, 1995.

[6] LAW, B.C., trans. *The Debates Commentary*. The Pali Text Society, 1940.

[7] NORMAN, K.R. *Collected Papers II*. The Pali Text Society, 1991.

[8] RHYS DAVIDS, T.W., trans. *Dialogues of the Buddha*. Vol. I. Dialogues of the Buddha: Translated from the Pali of the Dīgha Nikāya. Motilal Banarsidass, 2000.

6.5 Texts rejected by some

Discussions of authenticity in the ancient texts reveals that some in ancient times reached conclusions similar to those of modern scholars.

Authenticity is not a modern notion. It was central to the early community's understanding of its own religion, and the authenticity of certain texts is questioned in the traditions. These texts are among those considered by modern authorities as late additions. Texts rejected by various schools include:

1. According to the Sinhalese chronicle the Dīpavaṁsa (5.37 of Oldenberg's translation), the Mahāsāṅghika rejected the Parivāra (the last book of the Pali Vinaya Piṭaka), the six books of the Abhidhamma (six, because this is said to have occurred before the composition of the Kathāvatthu), the Paṭisambhidāmagga, the Niddesa, and some of the Jātakas.

2. According to the Pali Abhidhamma commentary, a student was of the opinion that the Abhidhamma was not spoken by the Buddha.[17]

[17] *'Abhidhammo kena bhāsito'ti? 'Na eso buddhabhāsito'ti*, "Who spoke the Abhidhamma?" "It was not spoken by the Buddha." (As 28,20)

This was refuted based on the occurrences of the word *abhidhamma* in the Vinaya. However, this shows that these parts of the Vinaya are late rather than showing that the Abhidhamma is early [1, §37].

3. Several Chinese monks around the 5th century rejected some or all of the Mahāyāna Sūtras: Hui-tao doubted the Pañcaviṁśatisāhasrikā Prajñāpāramitā Sūtra; T'an-le disparaged the Lotus Sūtra; Seng-yuan belittled the Mahāyāna Mahāparinirvāna Sūtra [3, 124].

4. The Sautrāntikas rejected the Abhidhamma [2, 181].

References

[1] HINÜBER, Oskar VON. *A Handbook of Pāli Literature.* Indian philology and South Asian studies. Walter de Gruyter, 2000.

[2] LAMOTTE, Étienne. *History of Indian Buddhism: From the Origins to the Śaka Era.* Publications de l'Institut orientaliste de Louvain. Université catholique de Louvain, Institut orientaliste, 1988.

[3] MIZUNO, Kogen. *Buddhist Sutras: Origin, Development, Transmission.* Kosei, 1982.

CHAPTER 7

Theoretical considerations

7.1 Scientific characteristics

The theory of authenticity has many characteristics of a scientific theory, which the theory of inauthenticity lacks.

While there is no complete agreement on what constitutes a scientific theory, there are a number of well-recognised characteristics [2] [4]. The theory that the EBTs are authentic (TOA—Theory of Authenticity) fulfils these criteria, while the theory that the EBTs are inauthentic (TOI—Theory of Inauthenticity) does not.

1. **Falsifiability:** The TOA may be easily falsified; that is, it is a "risky" theory in Popperian terms. For example, a single epigraphic reference to a Mahāyāna Sūtra dated to the 4th or 5th century BCE would conclusively refute the TOA. On the other hand, it is not easy to see how the TOI could be falsified, even in principle, still less in practice. Such theorists argue that "we do not know", or that "the evidence may be incomplete", or that there may have been a "systematic removal" of texts. Since all empirical knowledge is uncertain, incomplete, or subject to distortion, such objections can never be finally refuted.

2. **Plasticity:** A good theory is refined and improved when new evidence or arguments come to light. The TOA has repeatedly done this. Examples include the date of the historical Buddha, whether Pali

was his language, and whether the original texts were the same as the Pali, an unknown Ur-Canon, or a more loosely defined body of texts.

By contrast, proponents of the TOI, despite repeated criticism by experts in the field, have not substantially changed or adapted their arguments.

3. **Predictive power:** [6] The TOA has accurately predicted many subsequent developments in the field. A dramatic example is the statement by Samuel Beal in 1882: "... when the Vinaya and Āgama collections are thoroughly examined, I can have little doubt we shall find most if not all the Pali Suttas in a Chinese form." [1, XIII] This has been thoroughly substantiated by over a hundred years of comparative studies.

   Another example is the archaeological discoveries by Alexander Cunningham. He did not have the Pali or other EBTS available to him, but using the Greek sources, the Hindu Purāṇas, and especially the work of the Chinese pilgrim Xuanzang as his guide, he was able to locate many of the sites referred to in the EBTS. While more detailed work has necessitated subsequent revision of some of his findings, he was able to successfully map out the overall geography of ancient India, and most of his relevant identifications have been confirmed by positive archaeological identifications.

   A further example is the relative dating of the books of the Pali canon by Rhys Davids, a list that has been mostly corroborated by subsequent studies.[1] This is not just true of the overall picture, but of many details. One example is the question of the minor class of Vinaya rules, known as *dukkaṭa*. Oldenberg, based on his study of the Pali Vinaya, firmly said that this category arose only after the Buddha, because the monks would not make changes to the original classes of offences [3, XIX–XX]. At the time, comparative study of the Vinaya was still in its infancy, and Oldenberg would not have known that the Mahāsāṅghika Vinaya entirely lacks the category of *dukkaṭa*, but has the term *vinayātikrama* in a similar role.

---

[1] See section 3.8 above.

The TOI, on the other hand, has never predicted any major discoveries.

4. **Fecundity:** The TOA has been a highly fecund theory, that is, it has resulted in multiple further developments and discoveries. These include the reconstruction of ancient Indian history, the establishment of Indian archaeology, and the historical understanding of the relations between and development of the Buddhist texts of the various schools and languages. In addition to these purely academic results, the theory has inspired a spiritual resurgence in traditional and new Buddhist cultures.

   By contrast, the TOI has not resulted in any significant practical or theoretical developments. Its main impact seems to have been the disparagement of any study of Early Buddhism as useless because "we don't know". This has resulted in the neglect of the field, despite the very large amount of basic work that still needs to be done, as very many early texts have never been translated or adequately studied. This sterility has impacted on a variety of related specialities, such as archaeology, philosophy, and psychology, where non-specialists have been led to believe that the authenticity of the EBTs has been conclusively refuted, and therefore that there is no value in even trying to study them.

5. **Simplicity:** A good theory is able to account for a large number of facts with a small number of assumptions. The TOA is based on the simple, rational assumption that the EBTs attributed to the Buddha were largely spoken by him, unless there are good reasons to believe otherwise. With this simple starting point we are able to trace in a meaningful way the development of Buddhism.

   By way of comparison, it is difficult to work out exactly how the TOI proposes to explain the existence of the Buddhist texts. Sometimes the TOI theorists seem to imply that the texts were composed by later generations of monks, but mostly they claim the question is uncertain, which is, of course, a non-theory.

6. **Extensiveness:** The TOA encompasses a very wide range of facts known about Early Buddhism, as we have demonstrated throughout. By contrast, the TOI scholars have only considered a tiny fraction of the relevant evidence.

7. **Coherence:** The TOA is internally consistent, and does not violate any normal scientific or common sense principles. The TOI, on the other hand, sometimes asks us to believe that ancient monks invented a vast doctrinally and historically stratified literature for their own selfish interests.

8. **Responsiveness:** A good theory is not an isolated set of concepts; it lives in a constant climate of give and take, listening to critiques seriously and responding to them meaningfully. We have cited some examples of this above, such as the article by B. C. Law that responds to, corrects, and improves on Rhys Davids' chronological list of Pali texts. Another example is the study by Noble Ross Reat of the Śālistamba Sūtra. Earlier, the sceptical scholar Edward Conze had argued that we can only accept as authentic teachings that are shared between the Mahāsāṅghika and Sthavira groups of schools. Reat took up the challenge and was able to meet Conze's criterion [5, XI].

   While the TOI theorists have engaged in debate, this remains essentially superficial, since the theoretical mood of the TOI precludes acceptance of any genuine knowledge of the period.

References

[1] BEAL, Samuel. *Abstract of Four Lectures On Buddhist Literature in China.* BiblioLife, 2010. URL: http://archive.org/details/cu31924023158607.

[2] BOERSEMA, David. *Inductivism, Naturalism, and Metascientific Theories.* 1997. URL: http://www.bu.edu/wcp/Papers/Scie/ScieBoer.htm.

[3] OLDENBERG, H., ed. *Vinaya Piṭaka.* Pali Text Society, 1879–1883.

[4] RATIONALWIKI. *Scientific theory—RationalWiki.* Accessed 30-March-2013. URL: http://rationalwiki.org/w/index.php?title=Scientific_theory&oldid=1143715.

[5] REAT, Noble Ross, trans. *The Śālistamba Sūtra.* Motilal Banarsidass, 1993.

[6] THORNTON, Stephen. "Karl Popper". In: *The Stanford Encyclopedia of Philosophy*. Ed. by ZALTA, Edward N. Spring. 2013. URL: http://plato.stanford.edu/archives/spr2013/entries/popper/.

7.2 The character of inductive theories

The TOA is grounded on a wide range of facts, from which it draws a set of explanatory principles that have stood the test of time.

The TOA is similar to inductive theories in the classical sense, that is, it uses observation of particulars to test, correct, and improve general hypotheses, which in turn suggest avenues for further investigation and research [3].[2] It attempts to account for the entire range of what is known about the period. The arguments of the TOI theorists, on the other hand, are based on theoretical positions, with only occasional attempts at providing corroborating evidence.[3]

Examples of inductive theories include the theories of evolution and global warming. One of the characteristics of such theories is that they are probabilistic, and hence much better at establishing generalities than specifics [3]. This problem is well known in the case of global warming: the theory cannot predict whether any specific day will be hot or cold, but it can say with a high degree of probability that there will be more and more hot days in coming years.

Similarly, while we cannot say with any certainty that any specific text was literally spoken by the historical Buddha, we can say with a high degree of probability that the texts as a whole stem from him. This distinction is one of the rhetorical fault lines in the discussion of authenticity.[4] Sceptics assert that we can't know for certain whether any specific phrase was

---

[2] In the present instance, our starting hypothesis is that the EBTs are generally telling the truth when they explicitly state that they were spoken by the Buddha.

[3] We will not be drawn into the theoretical discussions of the problems with so-called "naive inductivism". It is obvious that scientific theories are inductive, in the sense that they are tested and developed through observations. Whether this establishes their "truth" or not, or what the role of other factors such as intuition and the like play, is beside the point we are making.

[4] See for example Anālayo's discussion of Schopen in his *The Historical Value of the Pali Discourses* [1, 239].

spoken by the Buddha,[5] while advocates affirm that the doctrinal teachings as a whole must come from him. While the sceptical assertion is true, it is trivially so, and has no real effect on our understanding of the status of the texts.

References

[1] Anālayo. "The Historical Value of the Pāli Discourses". In: *Indo-Iranian Journal* 55 (2012), pp. 223–253.

[2] Reat, Noble Ross. "The Śālistamba Sūtra and the Origins of Mahāyāna Buddhism". In: *Tenth International Conference of the International Association of Buddhist Studies*. The Permanent Delegation of Sri Lanka to Unesco, 1991, pp. 137–143.

[3] Vickers, John. "The Problem of Induction". In: *The Stanford Encyclopedia of Philosophy*. Ed. by Zalta, Edward N. Spring 2013. 2013. URL: http://plato.stanford.edu/archives/spr2013/entries/induction-problem/.

7.3 The problem of specifics

It is easy to argue that "we don't know" about the authenticity of any specific phrase or text when faced with variations in the sources, but this imprecision in details obscures the larger truths.

Here is one example of this problem of specifics. The Mahāparinibbāna Sutta says that when faithful devotees visit the site of the Buddha's birth, they will reflect, "Here the Buddha was born." In Pali this is *idha tathāgato jāto ti* (DN 16.5.8). The corresponding Sanskrit text uses *bhagavā* instead of *tathāgata*: *iha bhagavāñ jātaḥ*[6]—different words with the same meaning. This passage seems to be quoted in the Lumbinī Asokan pillar, which however uses two distinct phrases: A: *hida budhe jāte sakyamunī ti*; B: *hida bhagavaṁ jāte ti*. The *ti* indicates "end quote". Thus one of the forms on the pillar corresponds with the extant Sanskrit text, while one is different from both the Pali and the Sanskrit.

[5] According to Reat, "in recent years the emphasis of Buddhist studies in the West has fallen upon what cannot be ascribed to earliest Buddhism—i.e. that virtually nothing can be attributed with any certainty to earliest Buddhism," [2, 140]

[6] SMPS 41.11: "Blessed One" = *bhagavān*.

On a word level these are all equivalent; they are common terms that refer to the same individual. We might distinguish *tathāgata*, which is normally used by the Buddha when he refers to himself, whereas *bhagavā* and *buddha* are used by others. This would correspond with a situation where the Pali form is that spoken by the Buddha, while the other forms are those spoken by others about the Buddha.

Still, the meaning is the same in all cases. Thus focussing on individual differences obscures the larger point, which is that several diverse sources, from Sri Lanka, Nepal, and Kashmir (and doubtless other sources not covered here) all contain the same phrase in the same context. The general inference, then, is that the early Buddhist tradition acknowledged the Buddha's birthplace, that early Buddhists were encouraged to reflect on this at the place itself (reflection being implied by the "*ti*"), and that the textual and epigraphic sources confirm each other. From this, and the reference to Asoka visiting *sambodhi* (Bodh Gaya), it is reasonable to infer that the other sacred sites mentioned in the Mahāparinibbāna Sutta were also places of pilgrimage from an early date, probably from immediately after the Buddha's *parinibbāna*.

These are not isolated or uninteresting details. They raise questions as to the nature of the worship of the Buddha, the extent to which he was regarded as a historical figure, located in time and place, the emotional attitude of the early Buddhist community towards the Buddha, as well as possible economic and doctrinal implications of an early practice of pilgrimage. If we simply dismiss the evidence on the grounds that it is uncertain, we lose the chance to learn meaningful things about the Buddha and his early community.

7.4 Denialist Buddhism

The sceptical arguments bear more in common with denialism than with science.

Critics of Early Buddhism have adopted a rhetoric of scepticism in order to dismiss the notion of authenticity. Their arguments are apparently intended to be hard-nosed and unsentimental, but when examined closely they are reminiscent of arguments by denialists of various types, such as those relating to the harmful effects of tobacco, creationism, or the reality of man-made climate change. Just as sceptics characterise the search for authenticity as "Protestant Buddhism", it seems appropriate to describe this form of scepticism as "Denialist Buddhism".

The unifying characteristic of the various forms of denialism is their insistence on extreme, unreasonable scepticism regarding any truth claims they oppose. The following quote is from a tobacco industry executive, but it might just as well describe the fundamental principle of the sceptics of Early Buddhism.

> "… we are committed to an ill-defined middle ground which is articulated by variations on the theme that 'the case is not proved.'"[7]

Denialist movements share a common intellectual ancestry, in that they appropriate elements of postmodern thought in order to marginalise or denigrate science. And they share an unmistakable "tell", by which they can be distinguished from genuine scepticism. Denialists purport to be about a certain field, but they make no contributions to that field. Creationism has made no contribution to biology; climate change denial has made no contribution to climate science; and Denialist Buddhism has made no contribution to understanding the Buddha or his teachings. Its effect has been to dissuade people from even trying.

There are genuine epistemological problems in the study of Early Buddhism; in that we can all agree. But to argue, as the denialists do, from epistemological uncertainty to dismiss the entire field, is to get everything backwards. To study Early Buddhism is to study the origins of one of the great spiritual movements of humanity. It is a topic of intrinsic interest and worth. Of course there are difficulties, as there are in any field. But genuine enquirers take the problems as a challenge, and figure out ways to solve the problems. That's how science works. You make the unknown knowable. You don't run away from the problem and dismiss those who are trying to learn.

---

[7] May 1, 1972 Tobacco Institute memorandum from Fred Panzer, a vice-president for the tobacco industry, to Horace Kornegay, the president of The Tobacco Institute. `http://legacy.library.ucsf.edu/documentStore/d/j/p/djp62f00/Sdjp62f00.pdf`

Diethelm and McKee have identified various characteristics of denialists [1, 2–4]. Below we show how these characteristics apply to sceptics of early Buddhism.

For examples of the sceptical point of view we use Gregory Schopen's *Bones, Stones, and Buddhist Monks*, which has probably been the single most influential book in Buddhist studies in the last generation, in some countries at least. Schopen advocates an essentially negative attitude, saying, "It is however, very likely that [the canonical texts] will not tell us very much, and this, perhaps, gives rise to the broadest generalisation that we can make." [6, 192] With this as its starting point, there is little wonder that this movement has produced little to help us understand the EBTs. The main product of this form of scepticism is doubt, and the main outcome of such doubt is to give up trying to learn.[8]

1. *The identification of perceived conspiracies (including belief in corrupted peer review and inversionism).*

   Schopen attributes the absence of rules regarding stupas in the Pali Vinaya to their "systematic removal" by the Theravādin monks. He argues that a couple of references in much later texts, and some in the Pali Vinaya itself,[9] indicate that there were rules regarding these matters in the Vinaya, and that their loss could not be explained by accidental omission [6, 86*ff*]. He fails, however, to give any convincing account as to how or why such a change would be made. Moreover, his evidence is easily accounted for [2, 141–143] [3, 197–208].[10] Thus on the basis of evidence that is to start with extremely thin, and which is easily explained by more simple means,

[8] Reat comments: "For many Western scholars, this position [that virtually nothing can be attributed with any certainty to earliest Buddhism] has become an indisputable maxim which justifies neglect of ... the Pali canon." [4, 140]

[9] The references in the Pali Vinaya use the term *cetiya*, not *thūpa*, and the normal meaning of *cetiya* in the early texts is a shrine, such as a tree or cave or the like, usually for a *yakkha*, but which gradually becomes a residence for Buddhist monastics.

[10] The later texts he quotes are merely examples of a common phenomenon where monastics say that something is "Vinaya", whereas it is actually a later practice that everyone simply assumes is in the Vinaya. This happens constantly in monastic circles, and in fact is more common than genuine citing of the Vinaya in a manner that an academic would recognise.

Schopen postulates a vast hidden conspiracy that was able to make major systematic changes to an ancient scripture without anyone noticing. Elsewhere he does not even try to gather any evidence, but merely throws out the suggestion that the texts have been "intentionally altered." [6, 191]

2. *The use of fake experts (often with the smearing of real experts).*

   Climate change denialists often cite "scientists" who disagree with the consensus on global warming. On examination, the scientists almost invariably turn out to be experts in fields other than climate change. Similarly, most of the hard sceptics come from a background of later Buddhism or Tibetan studies, while those who specialise in Early Buddhism or Indian studies generally tend to affirm authenticity. The supposed "protestant" bias of early Indologists is criticised [6, 13], but the denialists do not acknowledge their own biases as secularists, materialists, postmodernists, or academics. Everyone has biases. Appreciating a person's perspective helps understand their approach to a subject, but this needs to be done without dismissing reasonable arguments and conclusions.

3. *Demanding impossible standards for research.*

   Critics point to the absence of early manuscripts [6, 1, 3, 27], or the absence of specific details in the archaeological record, such as early evidence of monasteries. This parallels the practice in climate change denialism or creationism of claiming to refute the science by pointing to the absence of certain concrete pieces of evidence. These theories, however, like the TOA, do not depend on specific, singular proofs, but on the convergence of large amounts of supporting data for which there is no better explanation.

   Inference, when properly used, does not rely on a chain of uncertain claims, one after another, diminishing in probability when compounded; but on the convergence of multiple lines of reasoning and evidence that independently confirm the result. The cautious use of such empirical method is described by Rhys Davids: "... before drawing the conclusion that, therefore, the Nikāyas, as we have them, are older than the existing text of the Mahābhārata, we should want a very much larger number of such cases, all tending the same way, and also the certainty that there were no cases of an opposite tendency that could not otherwise be explained." [5, 166]

4. *Use of fallacy, including misrepresentation and false analogy.*

   Schopen rarely considers seriously the methods used by scholars of early Buddhism, and when he does he misrepresents them. For example, he says the cardinal tenet of the higher criticism is that if all versions of a text agree they must stem from a pre-sectarian tradition [6, 26–27]. This ignores the fact, which is a very basic one, that the main picture of Buddhist history in India was developed in the 19th century, before any substantial comparative work was done. Scholars used a variety of methods, some of which we have outlined here, to arrive at conclusions that have, by and large, been confirmed by later comparative studies.

We live in an era of unprecedented potential for the study of Early Buddhism. Internationally, more people than ever are interested in Buddhism. Emerging technologies have opened up entirely new ways of making texts available and analysing them. Much of the potential of the field remains virtually untouched. Most of the EBTs remain untranslated into English.[11] There has been little or no application of digital or statistical analysis to the texts, which surely must be a field that offers promising insights. When so much basic work is left undone, it is absurd to claim that we cannot know anything. We simply don't know what we can know. Early Buddhism is a field of study in its infancy, with a huge scope of texts and other evidence, and a tiny population of serious scholars. We need to be supporting innovation and opening up frontiers, not prematurely dismissing the very possibility of knowledge.

[11] The Pali canon has been mostly translated into English. However, only small portions of the Chinese, Tibetan, and Sanskrit texts have been translated in modern languages. As far as we are aware, the language with the most extensive coverage of early Buddhist texts is Vietnamese, which has the Pali canon, the Āgamas, and three of the Chinese Vinayas.

References

[1] DIETHELM, Pascal and MCKEE, Martin. "Denialism: what is it and how should scientists respond?" In: *European Journal of Public Health* 19.1 (2009), pp. 2–4. URL: http://eurpub.oxfordjournals.org/content/19/1/2.full.pdf+html.

[2] GOMBRICH, Richard. "Making mountains without molehills: The case of the missing stūpa". In: *Journal of the Pali Text Society* (1990).

[3] HALLISEY, Charles. "Apropos the Pāli *Vinaya* as a historical document: a reply to Gregory Schopen". In: *Journal of the Pali Text Society* (1990).

[4] REAT, Noble Ross. "The Śālistamba Sūtra and the Origins of Mahāyāna Buddhism". In: *Tenth International Conference of the International Association of Buddhist Studies*. The Permanent Delegation of Sri Lanka to Unesco, 1991, pp. 137–143.

[5] RHYS DAVIDS, T.W. *Buddhist India*. Putnam, 1903. URL: http://fsnow.com/text/buddhist-india/.

[6] SCHOPEN, Gregory. *Bones, Stones, and Buddhist Monks*. University of Hawai'i Press, 1997.

CHAPTER 8

Conclusion

We know when the Buddha lived, where he lived, who he associated with, how he lived, and what he taught. We know these things with greater certainty than for almost any other historical figure from a comparable period. And we know this because of the EBTs. All other historical and archaeological information about the period depends on the EBTs to make sense.

One of the distinctive features of the EBTs is the their careful and conservative attitude to knowledge. "Buddha", after all, means "Awakened", and the development of wisdom is right at the heart of the Dhamma. The Buddha did not just teach the truth as he found it, but carefully detailed the way to discover the truth, and warned against leaping to rash conclusions. When we hear words of caution against accepting anything on mere faith, we are hearing the unmistakable inflection of the historical Buddha's own voice.

The Buddha's caution in what we can know is, however, balanced by his optimism, his belief, confirmed by his own experience, in the human mind. We can know. Not perfectly, perhaps, but well enough. There is no point in seeking for some ultimate truth in the messiness of the world we live in. What we need is a practical truth, one that is good enough.

In the Sandaka Sutta, the Buddha points out the dangers in living the spiritual life based on belief in a scriptural tradition. He says, with his characteristic reasonableness, that what is passed down in tradition may be well learnt or badly learnt, it may be true or it may be otherwise

(MN 76.24). Only if a spiritual life leads to the ending of suffering is it of true value.

The point of establishing the authenticity of the EBTs, then, is not to prove that they are all true. It is to show that they are useful. Within the corpus we indeed find that some things are well learnt, others badly learnt; some true, and some otherwise. With some reflection and effort, we are able to discern these things. What remains is a powerful, clear, balanced, and profound approach to the spiritual life. This approach has been of benefit to countless people, and we believe that it remains so today. By encouraging the study of the EBTs, we believe more people will be moved to apply these teachings and test them in the only way that the Buddha cared about: to reach the end of suffering.